Inside the Rainbow
Volume 3

First published in Great Britain in 2024 by Piquant Editions

www.piquanteditions.com

British Library Cataloguing-in-Publication Data
A catalogue record for this book is available from the British Library

ISBN: 978-1-80329-011-9

Cover Painting: *Woe, Woe, Woe!* by Pieter Kwant (2022)
Cover design: Projectluz.com

This book was painted and written with Elria,
for

Dave & Heather, Josh & Lauren,
Barnes & Beth, Tim & Nomes,
as well as

Susie, Isla, Dougal,
Lucas, Ciara, Heidi,
Zahra, Ava,
Saoirse, Jonah and Hudson.

Very truly, I tell you, we speak of what we know and testify to what we have seen; yet you do not receive our testimony. If I have told you about earthly things and you do not believe, how can you believe if I tell you about heavenly things? No one has ascended into heaven except the one who descended from heaven, the Son of Man. And just as Moses lifted up the serpent in the wilderness, so must the Son of Man be lifted up, that whoever believes in him may have eternal life.

John 3:11–15 (NRSV)

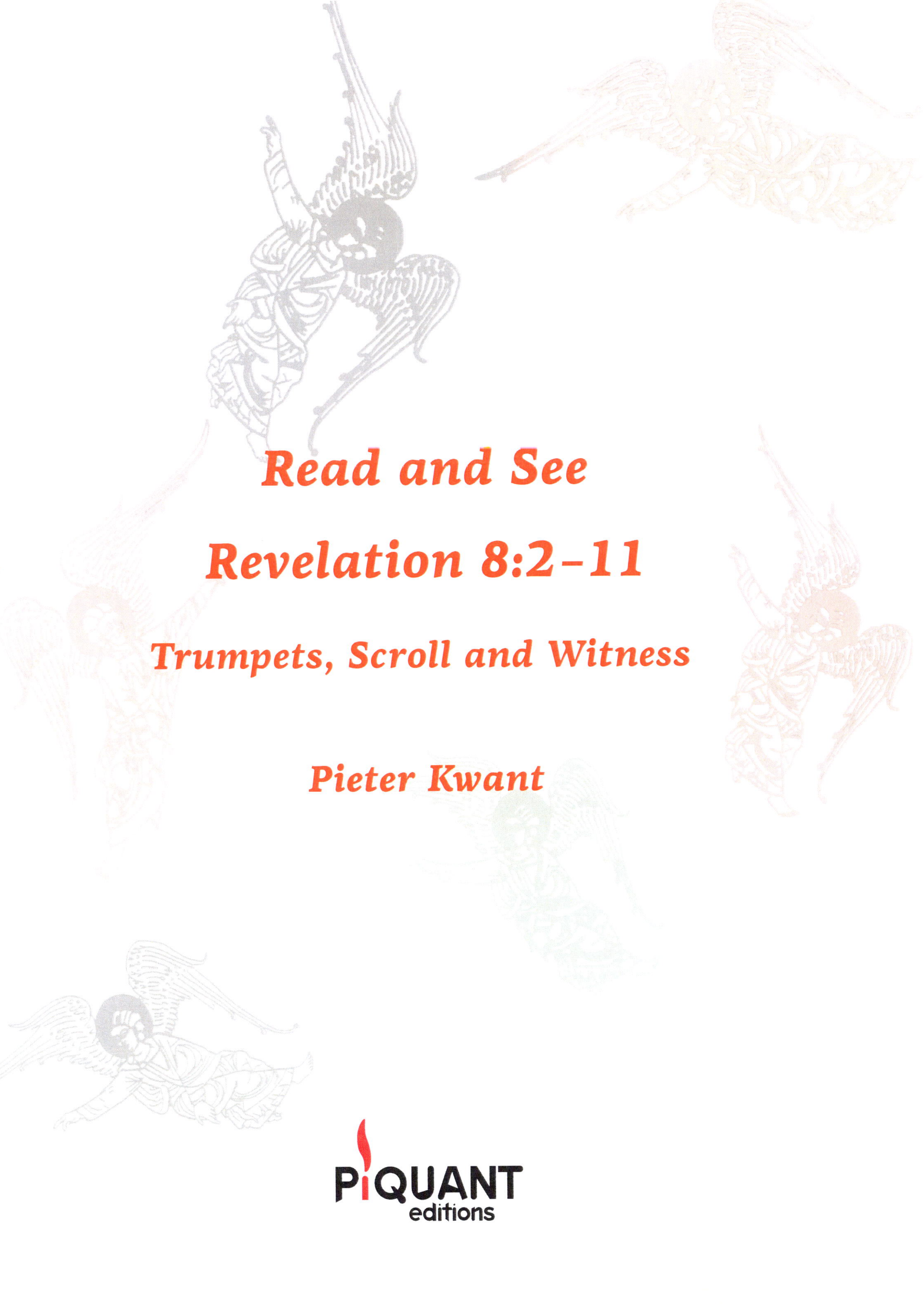

Read and See
Revelation 8:2–11
Trumpets, Scroll and Witness

Pieter Kwant

PiQUANT editions

Father Dunstan Massey

(16/4/1924 – 26/12/22)

It was with great sadness that we learnt of the death of our friend Dunstan Massey at a fulness of 98 years of age on the feast day of St Stephen in 2022. As a member of the Order of St. Benedict, he had laboured for over 70 years in relative obscurity despite being considered one of Canada's most original artists.

I first met Father Dunstan in 2000, shortly after we started Piquant Editions, through a contact at Regent College, Vancouver, who told me about this amazing artist-teacher-monk. Father Dunstan was ready for me with what we came to know as his characteristic sparkle, revealing a complete, meticulously detailed manuscript, handwritten in calligraphy, of an epic poem that traversed the classics, myth and Scripture in exploring the universal significance of the Resurrection, and animated by full-page ink and pencil drawings, the fruit of 25 years of work! Nothing about that project was vaguely "ordinary". *The Mystic Mountain, a poetic scenario for the Resurrection* was published in 2002. A 21-year-long friendship followed, sustained by a couple more visits and periodic correspondence. Classical literature and the Scriptures saturated his vision.

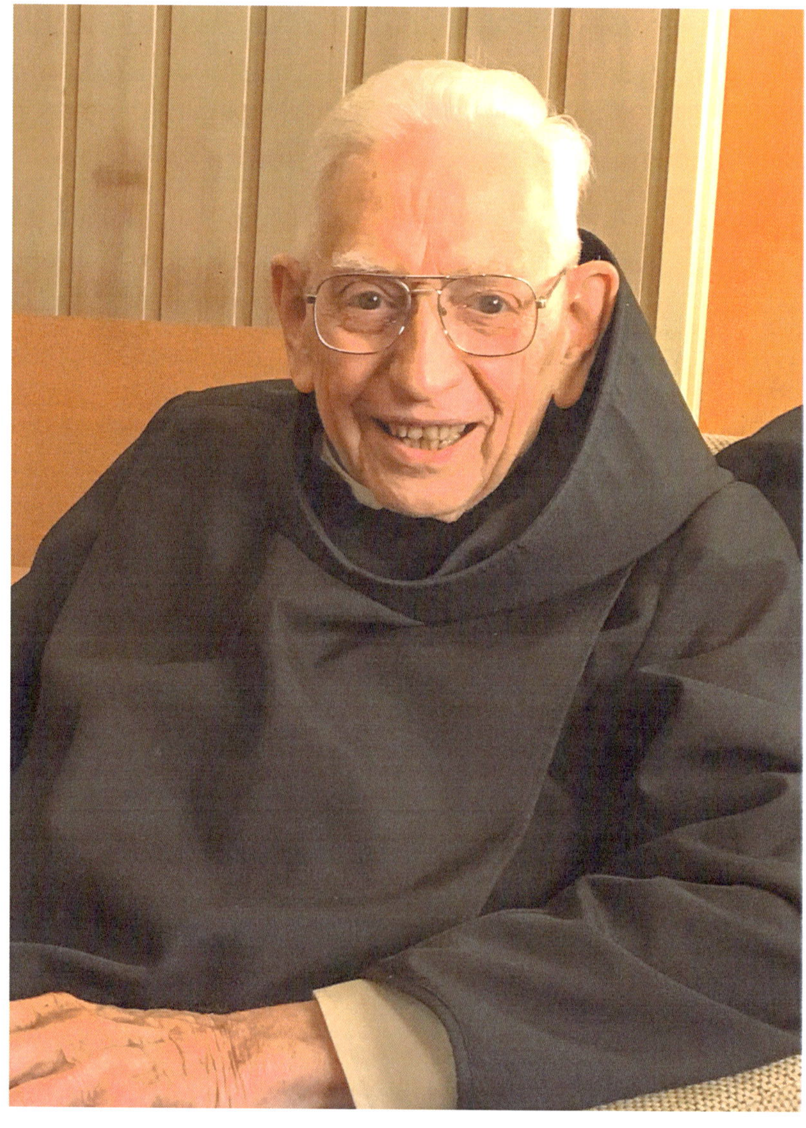

Receiving a letter from Father Dunstan was a highlight. It arrived in an A4, or larger, envelope and already must have caused much joy on its journey, because the envelope would be stamped from edge to edge with the most amazing collection of post stamps, colourfully arranged to cover every bit of the "blank page" around the address label.

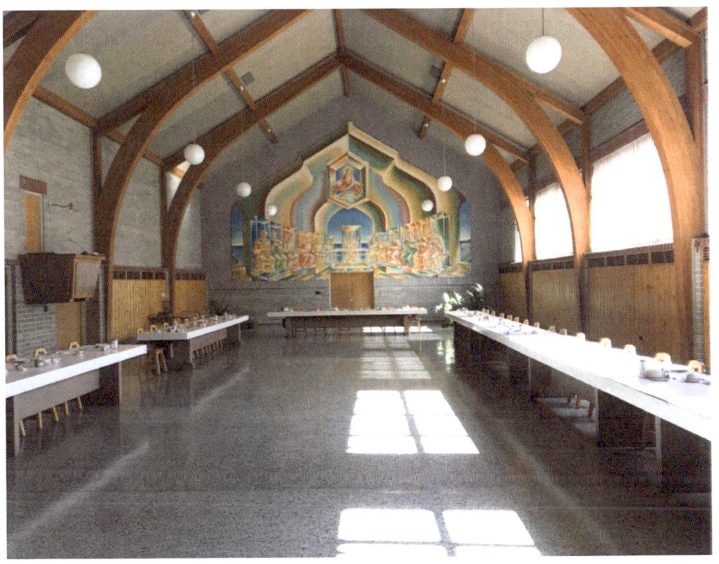

When my son, as a not very devout young person in his early twenties, visited Father Dunstan to film him in his surroundings, he came away enthusing: "He is the coolest dude I've ever met!" Dunstan's "sparkle" was infectious. He brimmed with life. In his letters he always included a description of projects he had in mind, and quite detailed progress reports on ones that he was busy with.

Father Dunstan had a brilliant mind, a fine sense of humour and a great love of the dramatic. He also had deep insight into human nature and was a determined worker, disciplined and intentional in what he did. It is no wonder, then, that he chose to specialise in a most demanding art form, namely fresco painting. Asking him once, playfully, what "workout" routine he followed, he smiled and replied he needed no workout, because in painting fresco he used every muscle in his body!

The decision that shaped his life and, by his own confession, surprisingly, enabled his unique art career, was taken after facing a crisis at the age of eighteen about what to do with his life. Already at sixteen years of age he had become the youngest person to have had a one-man show at the Vancouver Art Gallery and subsequently was feted by the likes of modernist Jack Shadbolt and the Group of Seven's Lawren Harris, as well as moneyed patrons. But on a retreat, reading and reflecting on Montalembert's *Monks of the West* and St. Bernard of Clairvaux's treatise *On the Love of God*, he heard God's call. Despite all protestations of art and music teachers, he decided to "throw my life away" in a monastic cloister! It was an unexpected decision, but his mother fully supported this vocation.

Much later, and with hindsight, he explained that had it not been for the efficient division of labour within the monastery, it would have been unaffordable for him ever to have become a twenty-first-century fresco painter! It reminds me of the wisdom of the protestant missionary Jim Elliot when he said, in relation to faith, "He is no fool who gives what he cannot keep to gain what he cannot lose."

Born William (Billy) Harold Massey, Dunstan chose his priesthood name after Saint Dunstan of Canterbury, patron saint of artisans and goldsmiths. He lived simply, playing his full part in all aspects of monastic life, and taught Classics at the Mission school well into his eighties. When celebrating his jubilee in the monastery and asked if he ever regretted not having "kept up" more with the world, he replied he did not need to "go to the world because the world comes to us." And when asked about his daily routines, he simply replied, "It is a steady rhythm of prayer and work, prayer and work..."

Father Dunstan hand-wrote his letters in beautiful calligraphy. When we asked if it would be possible to use email for prepress communications, he cheerfully replied it would be no problem. Next, an email arrived, with a scanned attachment, of a long letter in beautifully handwritten calligraphy! It is a joy to reread these letters. He often astonished us with the sheer size of the projects he proposed. At 80 he started on a monumental fresco for the back wall of the monastic refectory. He completed it in five years, but the preparatory sketches went back 35 years: *The Heavenly Banquet* was inspired by Leonardo da Vinci's *The Last Supper*, but with Matthias the apostle replacing Judas Iscariot.

When I saw Father Dunstan for the last time in Mission BC, two years before his death, I was not surprised that with a twinkle in his eye he showed me the drawings for twelve new, life-sized frescoes, part of a new Stations of the Cross.

His art, he once said, is meant to convey hope.

We rejoice that Father Dunstan completed the race. We remember him with deep thankfulness for the way his life and friendship illuminated God for us, and for his example of hopeful waiting for the day when Christ will come, when we will know, on earth, what we now "see" with eyes of faith only.

Come, Lord Jesus!

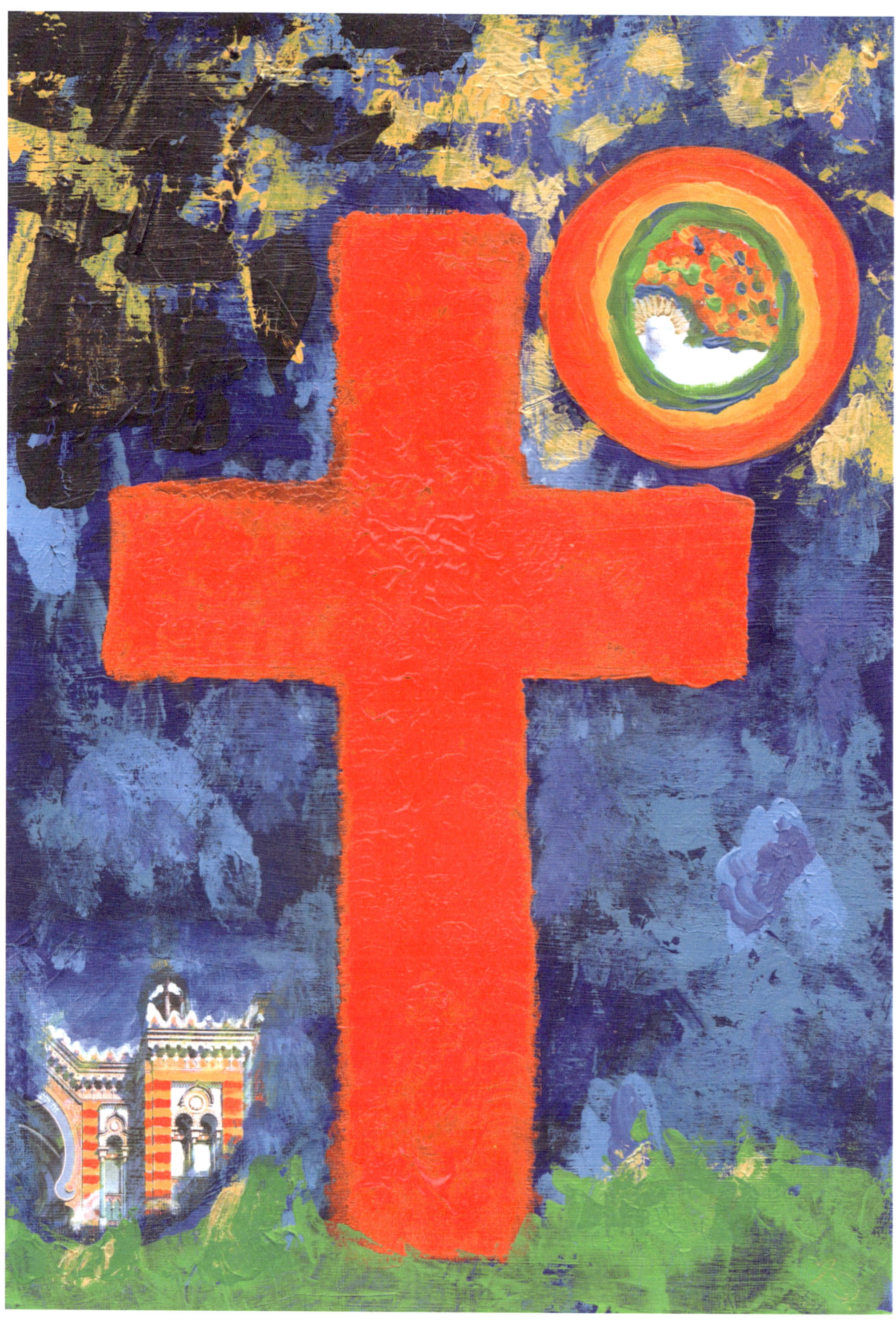

Understanding the Bigger Picture

While meditating on Revelation 11, I created a painting that I disliked because I felt it did not reflect the text adequately. Deciding not to throw it away, I started painting over it. To the left of the painting I kept the remains of the synagogue I originally painted, and to the right the remains of new Jerusalem. As the layers added up, a cross "appeared". While playing and praying like this, it struck me how the cross of Christ towers over everything the Bible communicates.

What about the cross of Christ in Revelation? I've come to see that in Revelation most things happen in heaven first and then on earth. But the crucifixion of Jesus happened only on earth, and it takes centre stage on earth and in heaven. Ellul, in his commentary, though I disagree with his universalistic conclusions, interprets the trumpets of Revelation as relating to Jesus in his death. I have come to agree with this, though I think it is only one layer of understanding Revelation.

Looking at my series of paintings as a whole, I was surprised to note that the Lamb has disappeared completely when we come to the trumpet series: not once is He mentioned in the "trumpet" chapters, yet I painted Him at every seal that was opened! This is an example of how painting enlightens understanding! Meditating on His absence, among other things, convinced me that those who hold to "recapitulation" as the organising principle of Revelation probably miss the point, at least as far as the seals and the trumpets are concerned: the two sequences tell different stories, though with some overlap.

The painting on the left also highlights how the cross separates the old, represented by the earthly temple and synagogue, from the new, represented by the circular rainbow and the presence of the Lamb, and distinguishes between the old and new covenants [more about this in Rev 11:19].

This change from old to new is one of the themes running through Revelation: ending of the old song and beginning of the new; ending of old Jerusalem and coming of new Jerusalem. Christ really does make all things new! In this Revelation may be more closely related to Hebrews than is generally realised, both in the discussion of old and new covenants, and in the presentation of Jesus. The movement from old to new culminates in the new relationship between Christ and the church (Rev 21 – 22). At least one aspect of the "big picture" is the ending of the old aeon and beginning of the new aeon: the old passes away (historically and spiritually), the new comes.

What am I learning from painting? First, when looking at illustrations in the early manuscripts we see the ancients found it challenging and often resorted to adding words into their illustrations. I have largely stayed away from inserting words but find readers need some explanation.

Secondly, I have found painting very helpful in forming my own understanding of the text. The process gives space for prayer while working. The physical process also helps me to focus my mind, which is more prone to wander when reading and reflecting abstractly. I do not try to make the most literal "picture" of the text, but search in my experience for images with similar allusions, which makes it very personal. Hence the need to also write in words. I hope a kind of recognisable visual language will develop, but it is not something I have predetermined or had as a goal. If at all, it will come from the doing.

Thirdly, my "quoting" from existing paintings helps me understand more about those works: for example, why an artist chose a particular image, and how they portrayed it. This is especially clear when comparing different manuscripts. In the Middle Ages, copying was the norm. The illustrators had the advantage of a common visual language, with defined symbols and conventions of portrayal. Today we do not have that, so quoting from contemporary images I need words to make my meaning clear.

Fourthly, my paintings have mostly been designed as book illustrations and function best in that way. I have found the exercise of painting in this way very instructive, and insights continue to arise with hindsight! That is a pleasant surprise.

Fifthly, I continue to have reservations about the usefulness of images in worship. These paintings are not intended for liturgical use. They attempt to present a visual "exegesis".

Sixthly, personally I have so far found the effect of the images as *aide-memoire* most helpful, especially for comparing sequential passages. Images are more memorable to me than texts. And obvious similarities or differences appear very clearly, which may be overshadowed by other matters when analysing texts.

Seventhly, my practice of experimenting with 7"x 7" abstract paintings on wood at the same time as making the pictorial images on canvas has paid great personal dividends. It has given me pure joy in self-expression, attempting to "say it" in colour rather than in form. My abstract meditations are valid approaches to the text, though often more difficult to respond to for viewers.

Tentatively, I conclude that the physicality of painting and then writing is helping me get closer into John's seeing and hearing.

The Incense of Prayer

In the silence following the opening of the seventh seal, John sees seven angels being given seven trumpets. In my painting I refer to them as the seven quoted *Beatus* angels, and to the seven trumpets as seven shofars, the most likely kind of trumpets John saw. We are introduced to an eighth angel, holding a golden censer. He is given a great amount of incense to offer on the golden altar of incense with the prayers of all the saints, and not just of the martyrs *contra* many commentators. This altar, prefigured in the earthly tabernacle, stands before the presence of God. So the Censer angel comes before God to draw attention to our prayers, having been given a vast amount of incense for that very purpose by God himself! And in this context, the seven angels prepare to blow their trumpets.

8: 2And I saw the seven angels who stand before God, and seven trumpets were given to them. 3Another angel with a golden censer came and stood at the altar; he was given a great quantity of incense to offer with the prayers of all the saints on the golden altar that is before the throne. 4And the smoke of the incense, with the prayers of the saints, rose before God from the hand of the angel. ...
6Now the seven angels who had the seven trumpets made ready to blow them...

To me this speaks of the mysterious significance of prayer. As I write, great cruelty is taking place in many countries. My friends are caught in Ukraine, Israel and Palestine, Lebanon... We pray for them daily. Often it feels such a weak and ineffective action in the face of overwhelming evil. But John encourages us to know that prayer motivates action from the very heart of heaven! God takes note, so much so that he arranges to draw his own attention to the saints' prayer through the incense, which apparently, he loves. [In the next Story we will see God acting in response to prayer.] Here God listens first to what we pray. I find this quite mind blowing and very encouraging.

It is surely right, here, to connect the specific prayers of the martyred saints at the opening of the fifth seal (Story Twenty-Seven), "Sovereign Lord, how long will it be?", with the prayers of all the saints alive then and now.

Who are the seven angels? They are unlikely to be the seven angels of the churches, but the number seven indicates a special group. These angels, fully available to do God's will, are possibly the angels of His Presence (Isa 63:9), or archangels, though the text does not explicitly state it. [We may meet them again later in Revelation as the agents of the seven last plagues.]

In the *Getty* illustration, below, you can see John peering in at the scene (I do love the way the *Getty* does this). The scene focusses on the incense before God and to the left of Him, and also on what happens in the next Story, the pouring out of the burning coals on the earth. The "censer" is depicted as the usual liturgical implement. God is seated on His throne: a person identified by His cruciform halo. He appears to be holding an unsealed book and is surrounded by the flames of the altar. To the right we see the cloud with the seven thunders, lightning, and an (earth)quake.

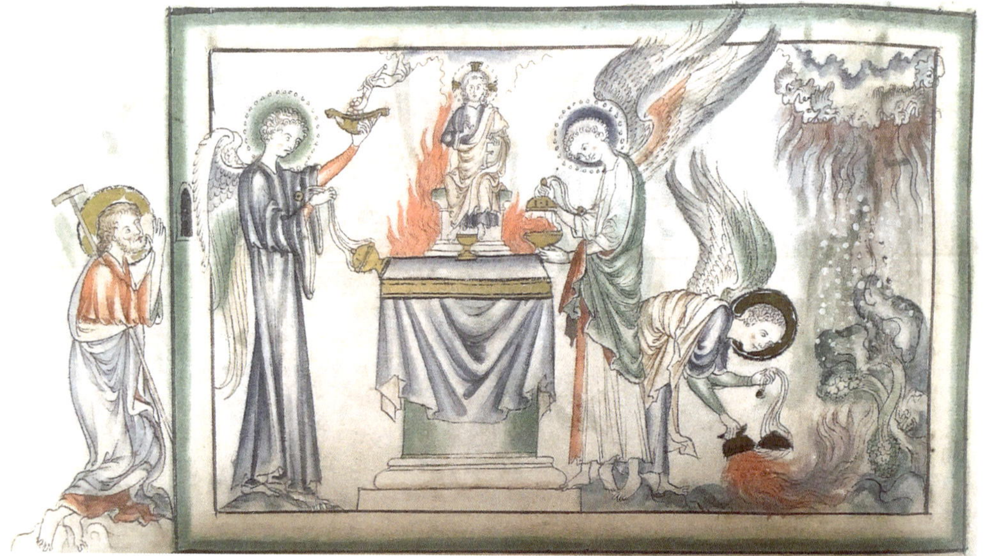

In my painting I focused on the incense and prayers rising in a blue (emerald) sweep before the throne of God's presence, which is symbolised by diamond and red sard. The olive background alludes to how this event in heaven closely relates to the earth (green).

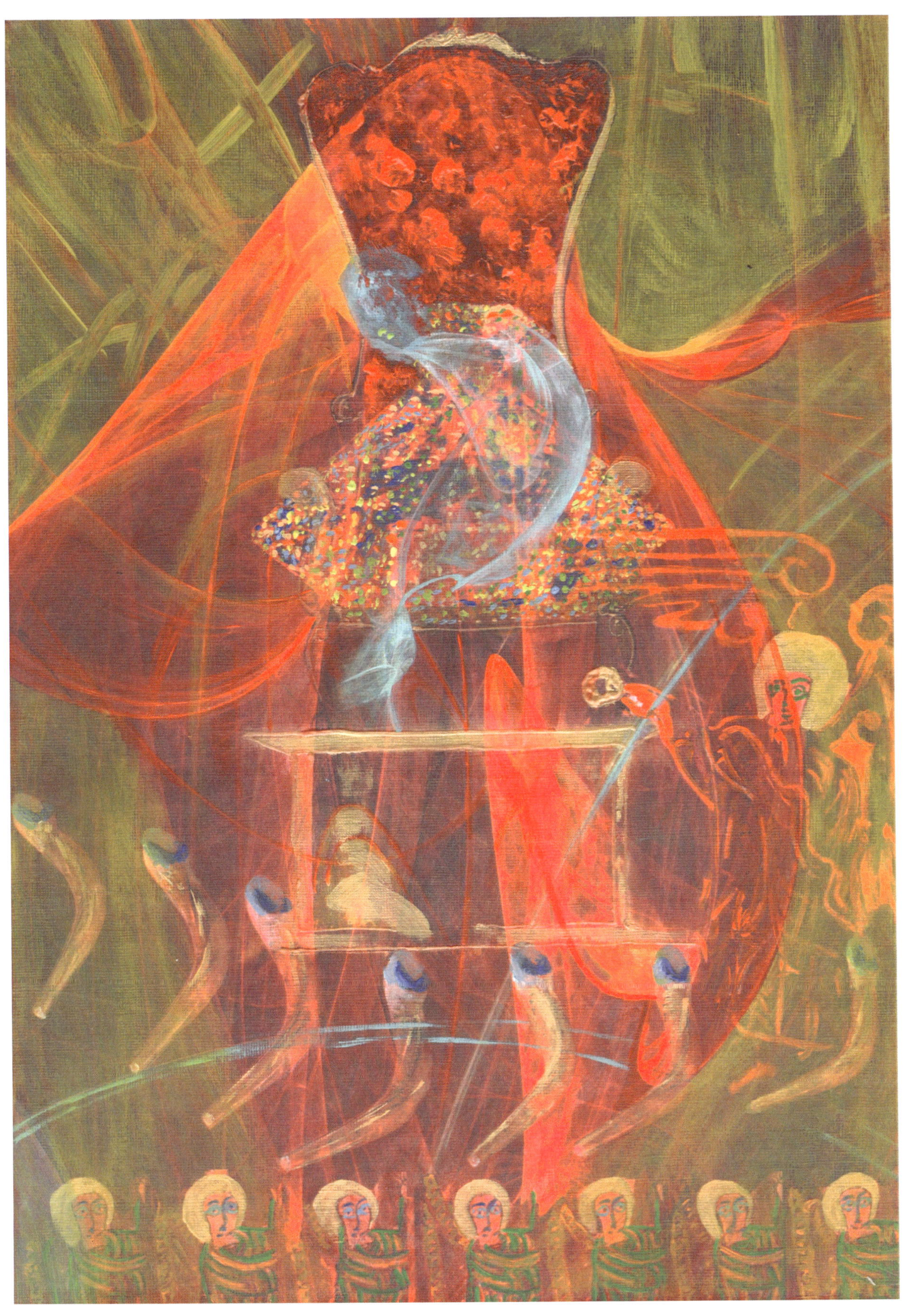

Burning Coals from Heaven's Altar

When the incense aroma and prayers of the saints have risen before God, the angel with the censer changes direction at the altar. He fills the coal shovel (not the liturgical censer this time, as Van der Waal convincingly shows in his commentary) with hot coals and fire, and flings them to the earth. Peals of thunder, rumblings, flashes of lightning and an earthquake follow (Lenski points out these are quakes, shakings, not necessarily earthquakes), with loud noise that I take as erupting on earth. Leithart and Jordan suggest the silence in heaven lasts until singing erupts again after the seventh trumpet.

8: [5]Then the angel took the censer and filled it with fire from the altar and threw it on the earth; and there were peals of thunder, rumblings, flashes of lightning, and an earthquake.

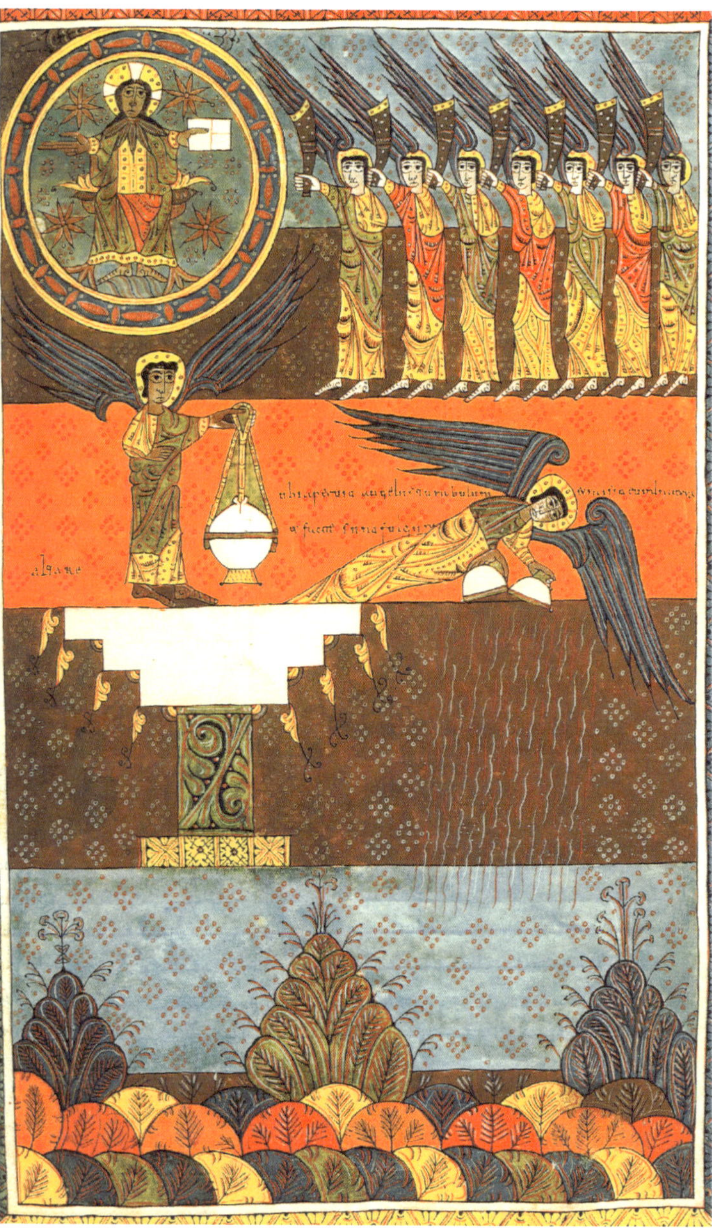

The action of the Altar angel leads immediately to the first trumpet call. In heaven the prayers of the saints are about to be translated into action on the earth. I agree with Bauckham that the Altar angel's action governs all the trumpet blasts and announces the coming of God in judgement. Bauckham also suggests an allusion to Sinai, especially when these phenomena are repeated in the last verse of Revelation 11, in the vision of the ark of the covenant.

The *Silos Beatus* illustration shows the now familiar layered medieval cosmology in the background. The seven Trumpet angels are in heaven next to the mandala (signifying a holy space) enclosing God, holding an open book in His hand. The Altar angel is shown in two positions: first he offers incense; then he throws the full contents to the earth. I love the way he falls down himself. Below, we see the earth, still untouched.

My own painting is much more dramatic. For me this scene introduces and summarises what will be accomplished by the seven trumpets. So, I painted a mountain of burning coals descending onto a shaking earth. The sky is filled with (thunder) clouds, and lightning forks in response to the action of the Altar angel. These signs indicate the intention of what will follow: God's judgement has begun, for the mountain of burning coal from heaven starts a fire that will be impossible to extinguish.

Heaven is answering the heart cries and prayers of the martyrs and all the living saints. God, who heard, now acts to bring justice through judgement. [As we shall see, there is still hope for the people of the earth to turn from their ways.] The first four trumpet warnings target believers and unbelievers alike. The people of God who still associate with those taking their stand against God must repent, as the churches were warned to do in Revelation 2 and 3.

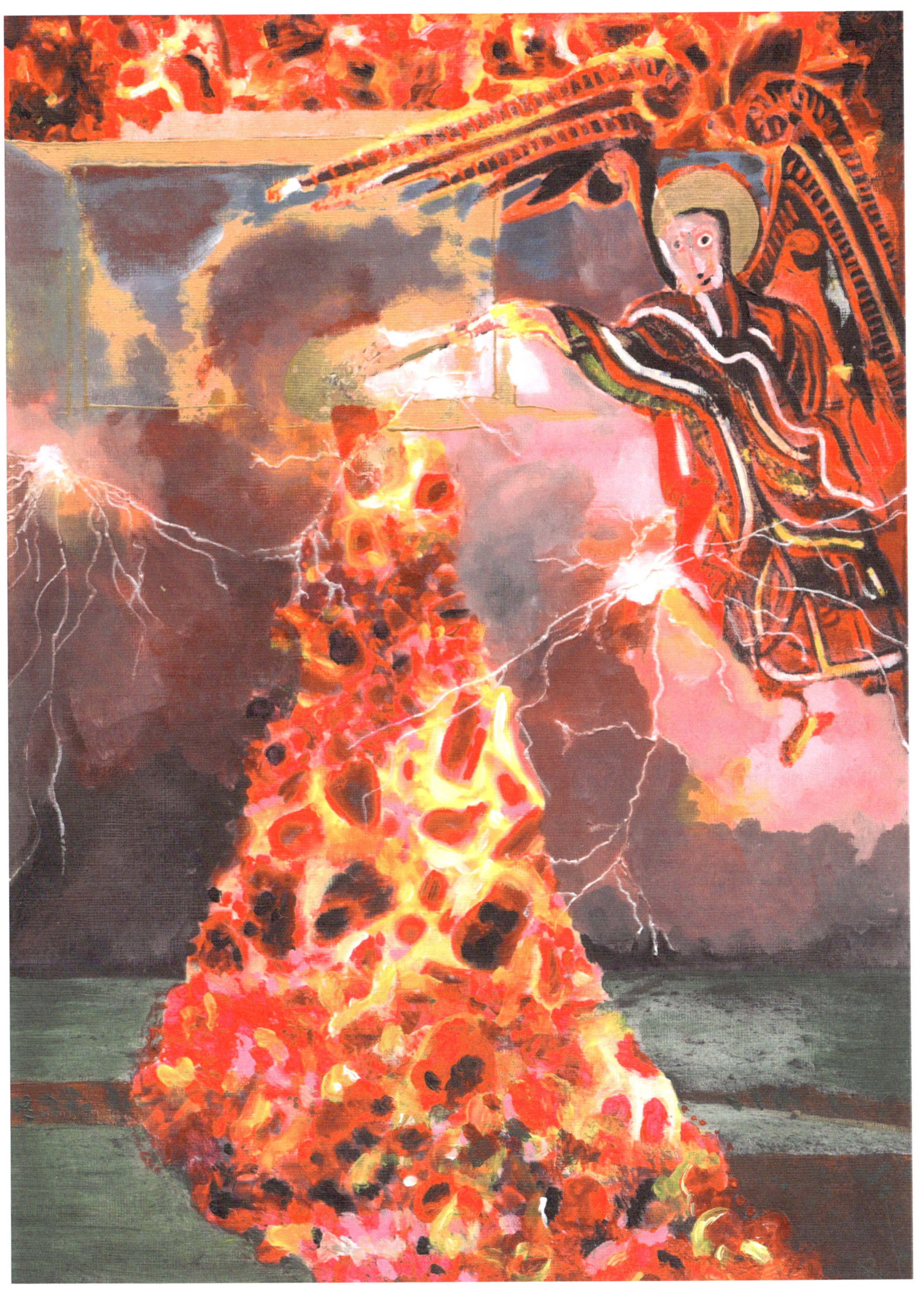

The First Trumpet

We are still in John's vision when the first trumpet sounds in heaven. A trumpet-like voice (1:10) announced the opening vision of Christ. Now John hears a real trumpet sound. The result on earth is hail and fire mingled with blood, with a third of the earth burnt up, and a third of the trees and of the grass. The action moves from heaven to earth. But this judgement on earth is different from, and more severe than, what followed the opening of the seals.

The *Rylands Beatus* depicts this in a rather literal way, across the cosmic levels, from heaven to earth, and on earth affecting trees and grass.

I painted this vision very dramatically, as I tried to visualize "a third" being destroyed by fire. I picture a shofar, altar and shovel at the top, to remind us of the visionary context. A strange combination of hail and fire falls, followed by blood.

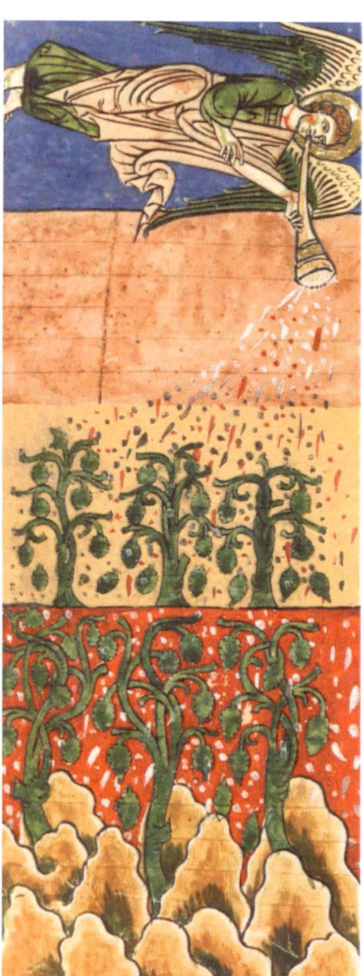

The sound of trumpets signals decisive action in war and worship, as in the OT, for example, the trumpet calls around Jericho and Mount Sinai (Exod 19:6).

How do we interpret this vision? The ancients understood this vision in spiritual terms, allegorising the sound of the trumpet as preaching. I prefer to start with the literal narrative, which appears to be a description in visionary language of God's judgement on the earth. The first trumpet initiates a kind of reverse creation, or de-creation. And all of the first four trumpets announce this. The first judgement is the partial destruction of the earth and its vegetation. The trumpets initiate supernatural activity, whereas the opening of the seals showed natural, though sad, consequences of the gospel entering.

> *8: 7The first angel blew his trumpet, and there came hail and fire, mixed with blood, and they were hurled to the earth; and a third of the earth was burned up, and a third of the trees were burned up, and all green grass was burned up.*

Commentators also try to link these events with the plagues mentioned in the sixth unsealing. That makes some sense. Both allude to the plagues in Egypt before the exodus. But the destruction here is of cosmic proportions.

Is there more? Leithart sees the earth as representing Israel, and the sea, mentioned at the next trumpet, as representing the Gentiles. Beale sees these plagues as typological or prophetic foreshadowings of God's judgements against unbelievers throughout the Church Age, culminating in the last judgement, which initiates the final "exodus" of God's people from this world of captivity to eternal freedom.

What is this blood that falls from heaven, and how literal is it? Some think nothing falls from heaven and blood results from what is thrown down to earth. Others suggest it is the blood of the martyrs under the altar, condemning those who shed it. Still others suggest, and I agree, that it is the purifying blood of Christ, which would make it a more miraculous and metaphorical downpour that cannot be taken literally.

Many commentators also see this first blast of the trumpet as being fulfilled in AD 70, in which case the earth is the promised land and the falling elements, the covenant wrath on God's people. Personally, I think we need to take a step back and apply this to Jesus and the judgement that fell upon Him first. After that, the judgement continues to rain down on the unfaithful, in Jerusalem in AD 70, then on the Roman Empire and many empires and evil cultures that follow, till finally in the "day of the Lord", which I believe is what this vision announces.

We could say that this first trumpet blast represents de-creation at the physical level, Christ's ordeal at the spiritual level and the present experience of believers united to Christ, and a physical and spiritual experience at the final judgement.

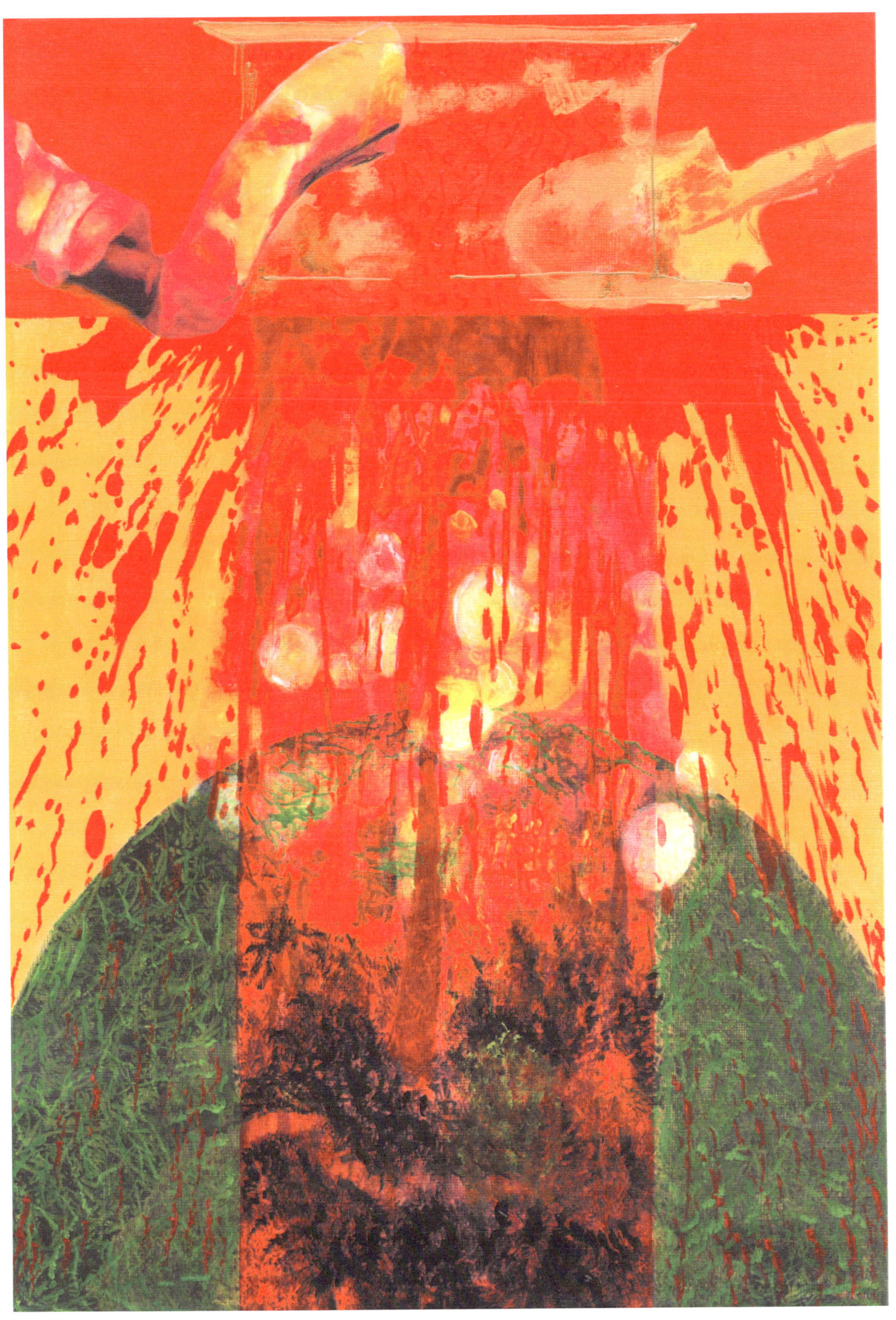

The Second Trumpet

When we hear the second trumpet, a great mountain is thrown into the sea and a third of the sea turns to blood, with a third of the living creatures and a third of the ships destroyed. So, we see the return of fire and blood, but in a different context. This continues the de-creation but now with God's judgement on the sea. (It also becomes clearer that the first four trumpets form a unit in their effect on the whole of creation.)

Looking back at the series of seven paintings on the opening of the seals (Stories Twenty-Three to Twenty-Eight), it was impossible to ignore the constant presence of the Lamb. But here, at the trumpets, Jesus is strangely absent. Instead, angels appear to be in charge of the action. Many commentators suggest that the incense represents the intercession of Jesus: it is what irresistibly alerts God to the saints' prayers.

What is this great burning mountain? Caird and Stefanovic see a reference here to Jeremiah 51:25, where Babylon is the great destroying mountain. They see this trumpet call as a foretaste of what will happen later [in the fall of Babylon]. Leithart suggests that this burning mountain is exactly the same as the burning earth at the first trumpet. I think that Stefanovic is right when he reminds us that mountains in the OT often represented kingdoms or empires (Ps 78:68; Isa 41:15; Jer 51:24–29; Ezek 35:2–3; Obad 1:8–9). So it could be justified to identify this mountain with Babylon. She is clearly being cast down into the sea, to be raised again from the sea later on.

8: [8]The second angel blew his trumpet, and something like a great mountain, burning with fire, was thrown into the sea. [9]A third of the sea became blood, a third of the living creatures in the sea died, and a third of the ships were destroyed.

The *Getty* pictures this scene very literally, as I did in my painting where I also introduced horizontal sections to depict the sequence and details of the vision.

I would see a threefold spiritual fulfilment here in the judgement that fell on Jesus at His crucifixion, which anticipates the further judgements on the kingdoms of this world that have set themselves against God (starting with Jerusalem and Rome). And finally judgement in response to the prayers of God's people that looks forward to the day of the Lord, when the last "mountain" will be thrown down

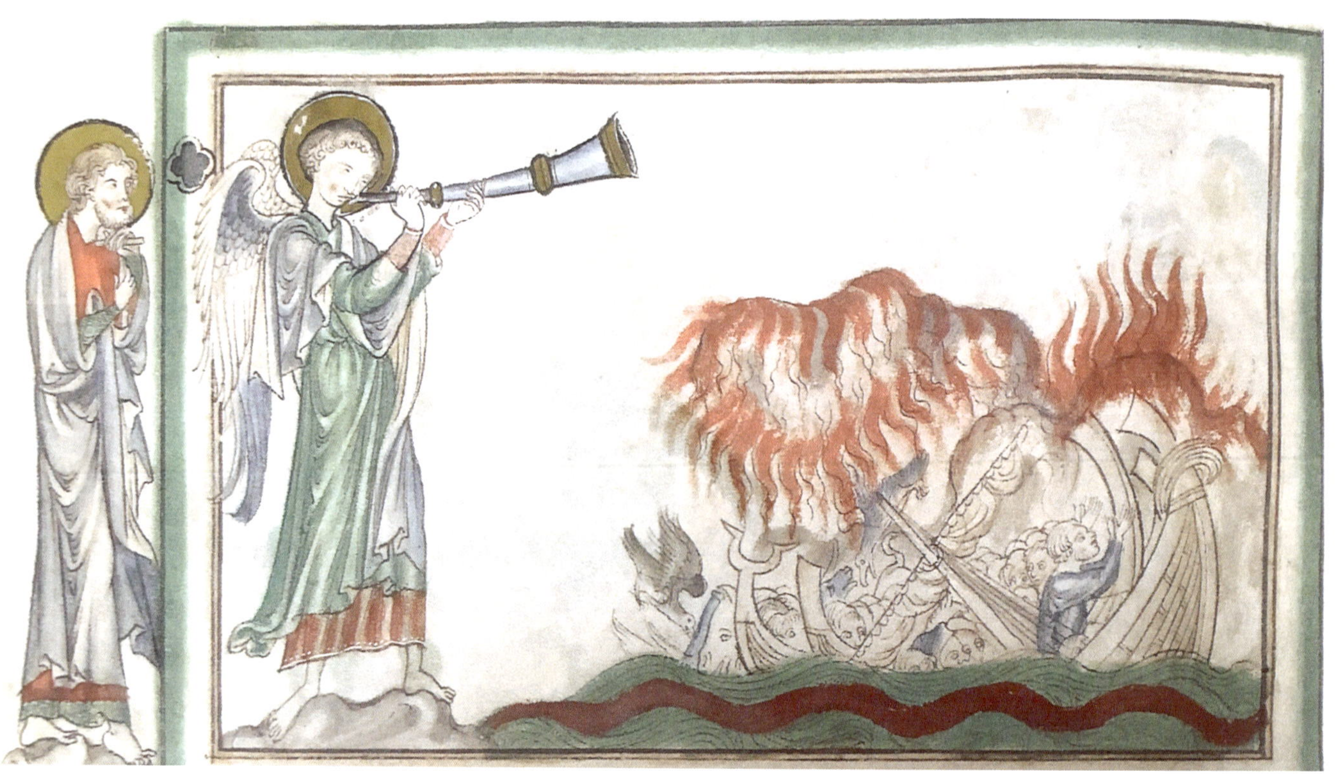

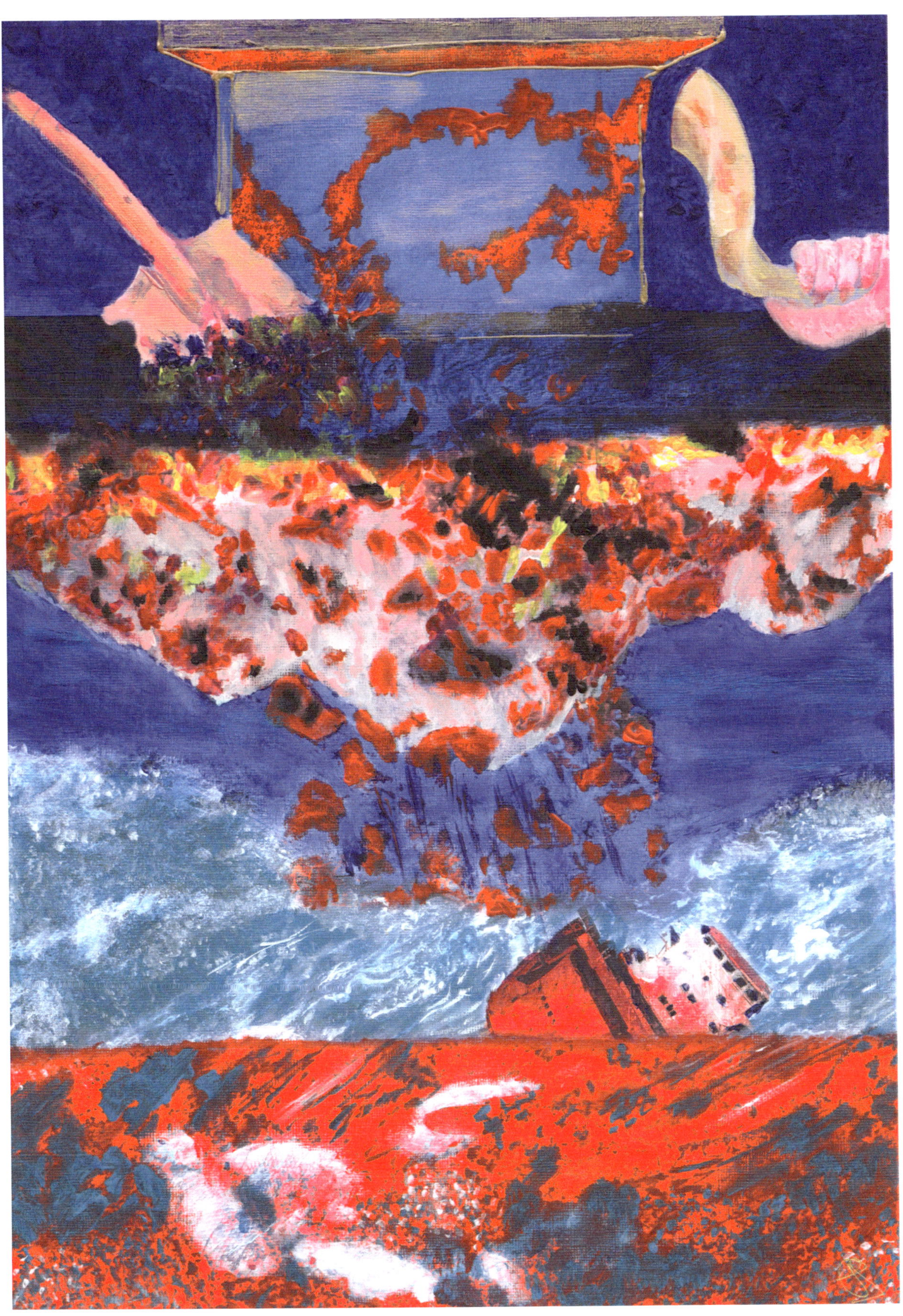

The Third Trumpet

This trumpet causes a great star to fall from heaven on a third of the rivers and water springs. We cannot take this literally. The star is named: Wormwood (a bitter tasting herb). When it enters the waters they become bitter. Unlike the effect of the medicinal herb, the result here is death for those who drink the water.

The *Ryland* below shows three layers of judgement. The star mid-air and the waters bring death to the earth. I quote this in my painting, but added more movement and realism. I struggled with the specific meaning of this third judgement. Painting it also did not help me much exegetically, but I was reminded that it is a reversal of the exodus miracle at Mara.

8: [10]The third angel blew his trumpet, and a great star fell from heaven, blazing like a torch, and it fell on a third of the rivers and on the springs of water. [11]The name of the star is Wormwood. A third of the waters became wormwood, and many died from the water, because it was made bitter.

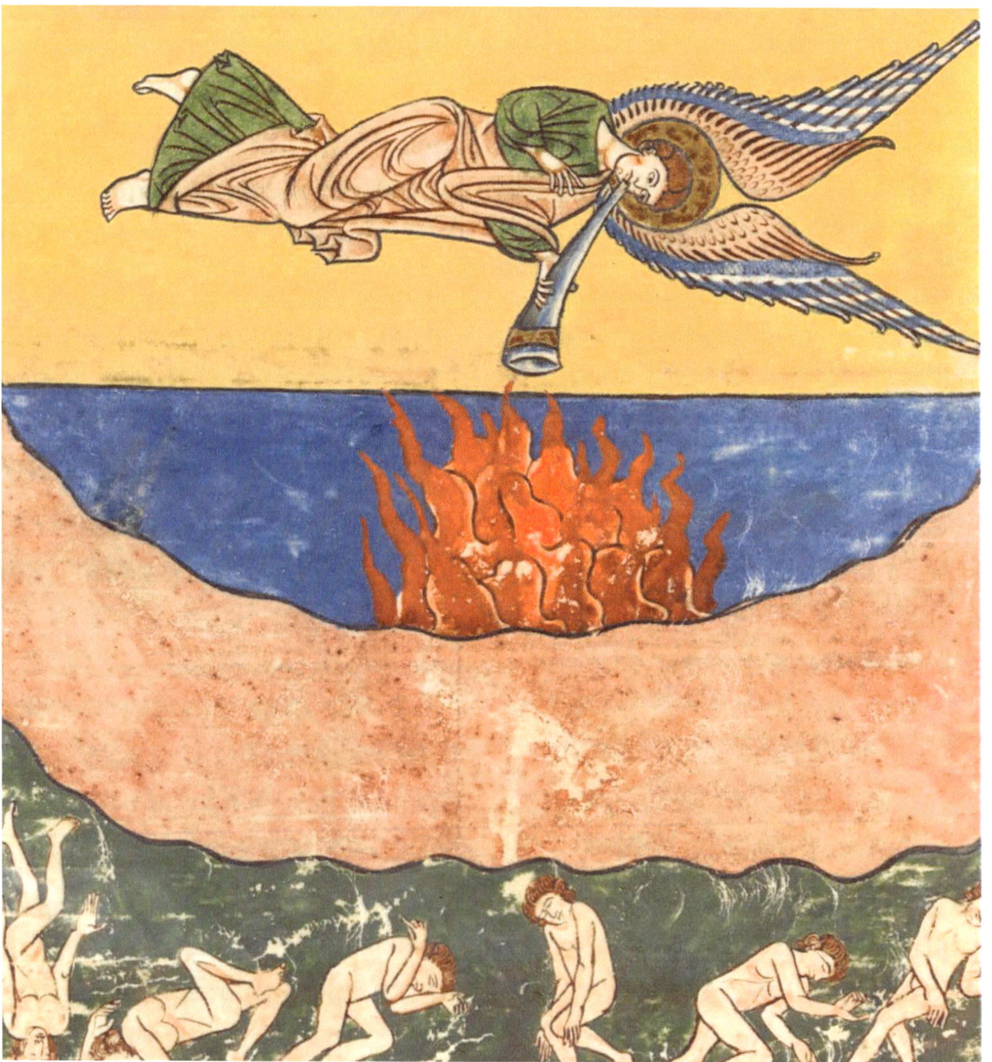

What does this star represent? At face value it is a cosmic event that causes a natural disaster, and many modern commentators take this view. But the name of the star suggests more. Caird suggests that Wormwood is the star of the new Babylon (Isa 14:12–20), which by her idolatry has poisoned the springs of her own life (Jer 9:15). Leithart suggests that shooting stars are failed rulers and nations, or broken clocks (Gen 1:14). He also suggests a satanic origin, pointing to one of the Herods. Stefanovic thinks this great star is a symbol of Satan himself (12:9); Tonstad also uses Revelation 12 to interpret this passage in this way.

I find it most compelling for this star to represent a failed ruler or angel, one who poisons human systems so that people die. This can refer literally to a ruler or power, over the centuries, starting with the rule of the Herods; or spiritually, as the ancient allegorists suggested, to particular heresy.

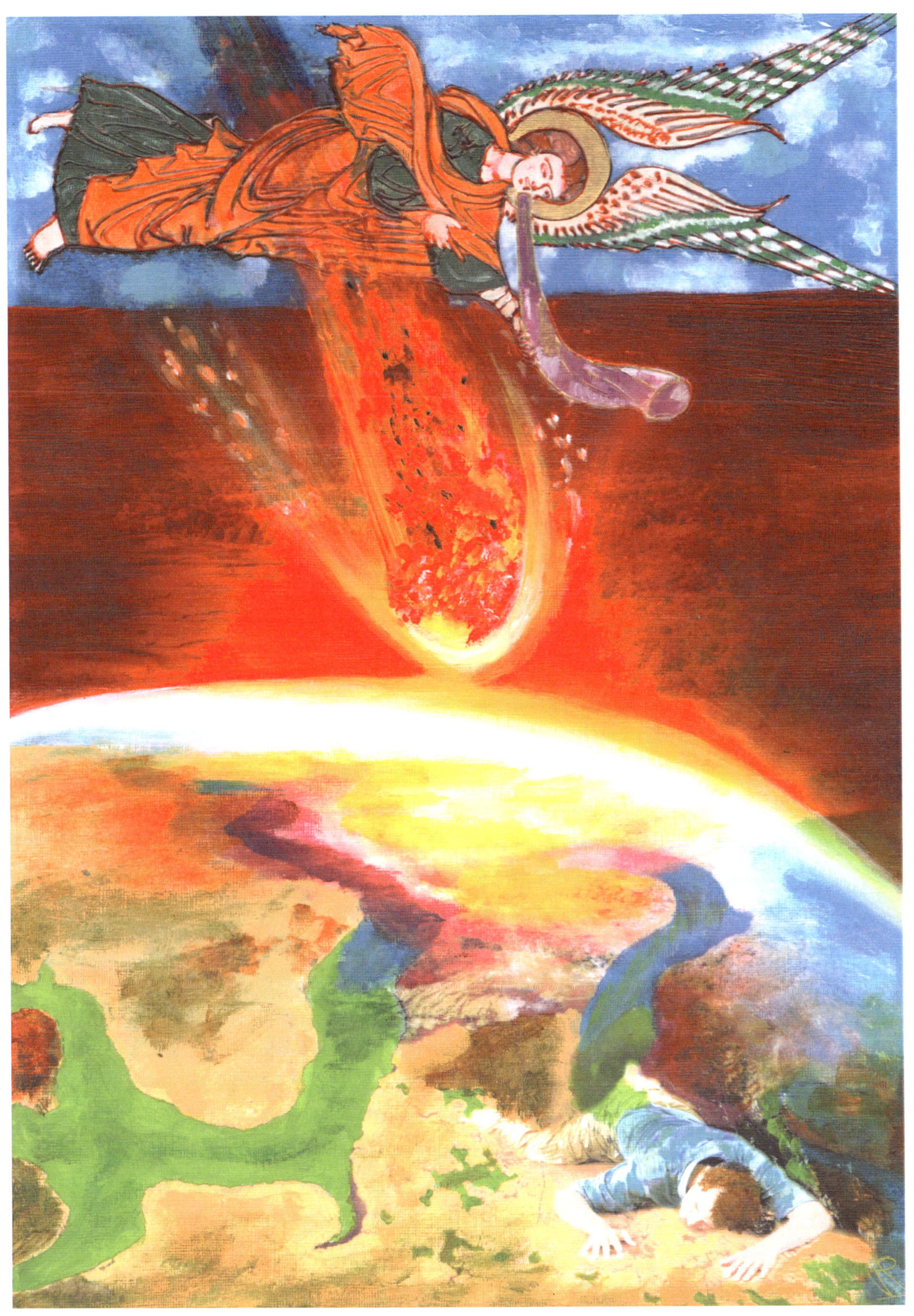

The Fourth Trumpet

A truly cosmic event of de-creation follows the fourth trumpet. This time it involves the sun, moon and stars. The "a third" is even stranger to visualise here if you take it literally.

The manuscript illustrations do not help much with our understanding here, but they are interesting and suggestive. The image from the *Silos* has a rather unique way of dividing the sun and moon into three parts. It also links this trumpet to Story Thirty-Nine, where the eagle, representing the church, hovers in front of the Trumpet angel.

In my painting I tried to divide the sun, moon and stars into three parts. At first, I did it horizontally, which looked very strange, but then Elria suggested a vertical division, which worked. The Beatus angel covers all three layers.

But what kind of judgement is this? The repetition of "a third" links it to the previous three trumpets. Leithart sees this as God's judging the political rulers and authorities. I think Ellul is right too, that this judgement is particularly directed at all the spiritual rulers and authorities in heaven, the "powers". So, it seems that on one hand God is judging political rulers and systems, and on the other, spiritual powers or principalities. In relation to the first, Stefanovic helpfully points to Ezekiel 32:7-8. In relation to the second, I think of the spiritual warfare against, and defeat of, the powers in which Jesus was involved on the cross, and the warfare in which the church is still involved, as in Ephesians 6. That battle is also linked to unceasing prayer, as it is here. God will judge the powers for all the wrongs they caused and are causing. Ephesians shows that our response can only be to pray without ceasing!

> *8: 12The fourth angel blew his trumpet, and a third of the sun was struck, and a third of the moon, and a third of the stars, so that a third of their light was darkened; a third of the day was kept from shining, and likewise the night.*

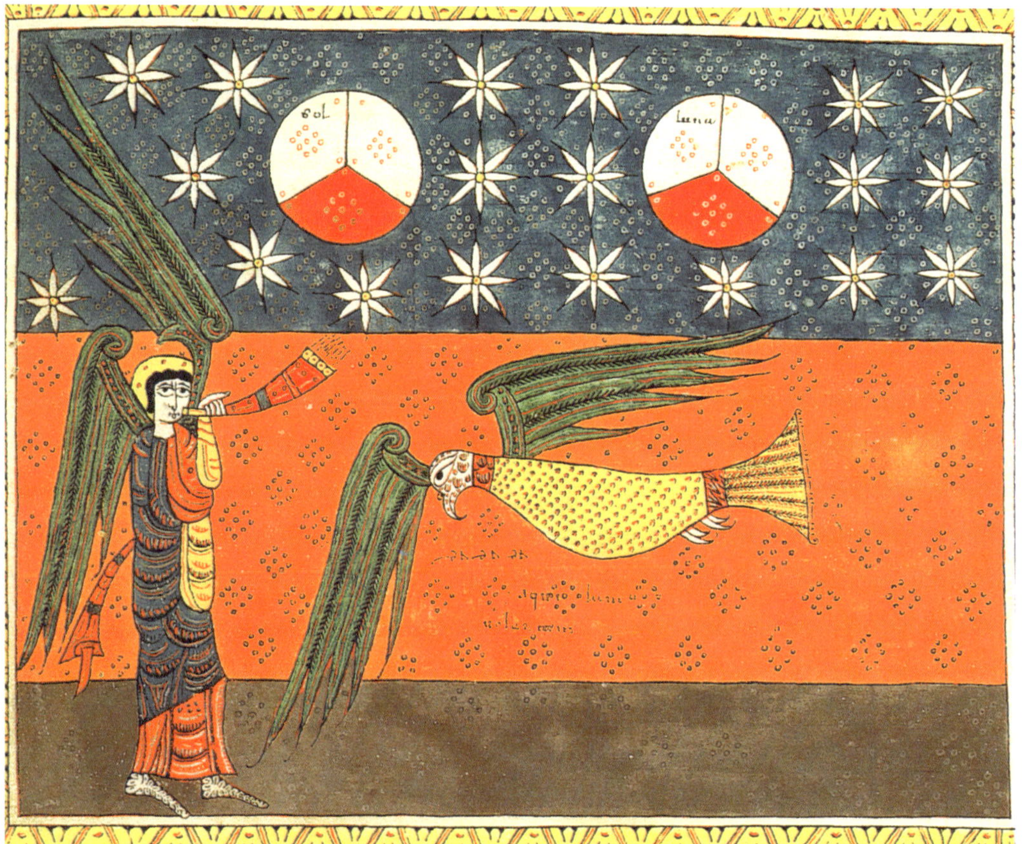

Why a "third"? As we have seen, it does not refer to a literal division. Looking back at the opening of the seals, there was a "quarter" influence. [Later, with the bowls, we will see the judgement of it all.] So, the "a third" here fits in a progressive sequence. Some commentators suggest it refers to the third of fallen angels cast out of heaven along with Satan (Rev 12). And some use this passage as a major interpretive tool. I have doubts about that. To me, it suggests a limited effect, not the full, final effect as yet, but terrible judgement all the same.

More importantly "a third" leaves open the possibility of repentance. All is not lost yet!

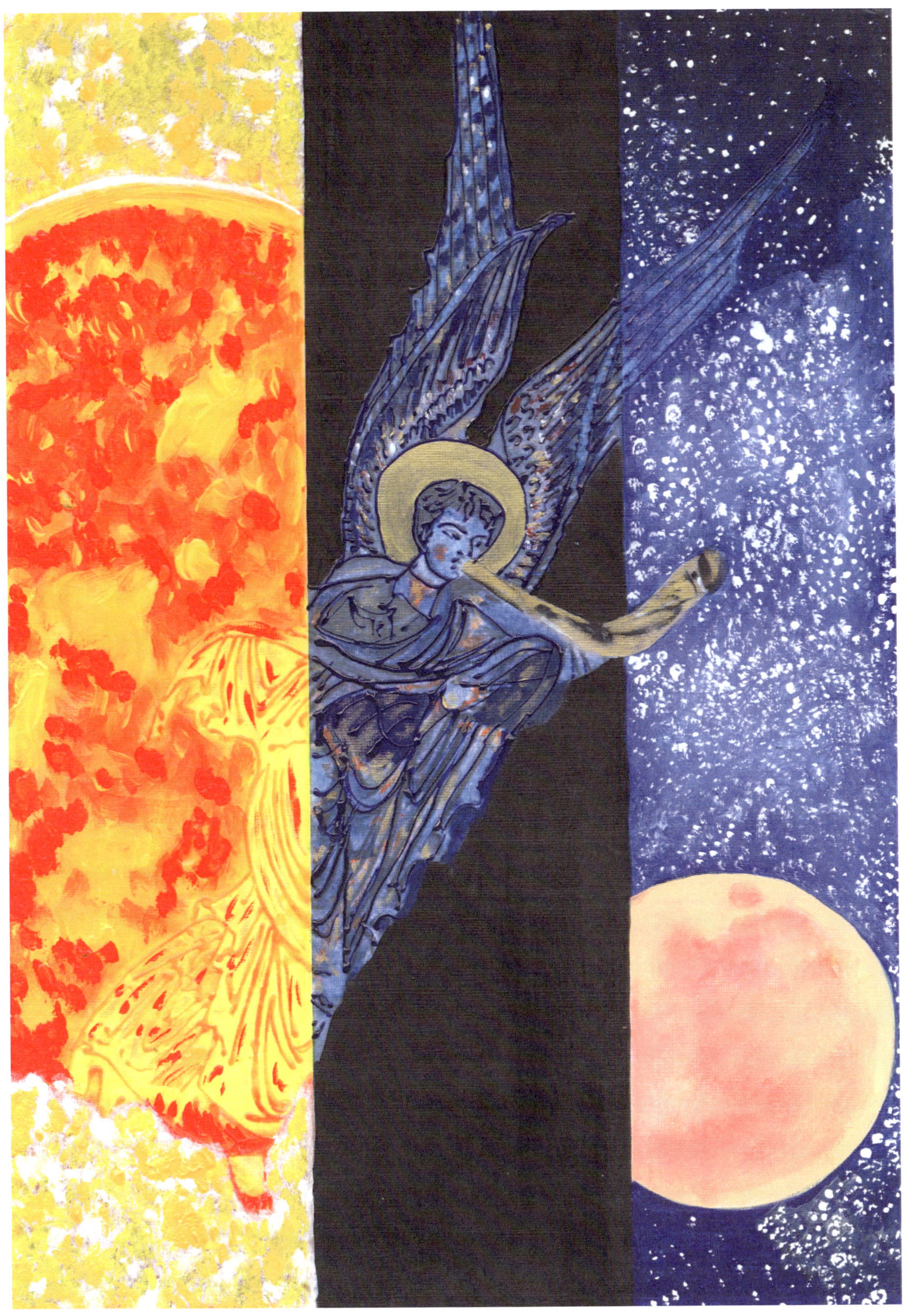

Woe, Woe, Woe!

> *8: [13]Then I looked, and I heard an eagle crying with a loud voice as it flew in midheaven, "Woe, woe, woe to the inhabitants of the earth, at the blasts of the other trumpets that the three angels are about to blow!"*

After the judgement on creation, we now come to more specific judgements of the inhabitants on the earth, previously identified as those against God, and separated from those sealed by God. Judgement here is reminiscent of the plagues in Egypt at the exodus, some of which fell on everyone and others only on the Egyptians. In this woe the action moves from general de-creation to more specific judgements on God's enemies.

In Luther's Bible of 1534, we see that Cranach chose an angel to announce the three plagues. Our biblical text identifies an eagle, which could also be translated as "vulture". Translators and commentators make their choices.

I chose to paint an eagle, an austere bird and powerful hunter that falls upon its prey unawares. It was the symbol used as the standard of a Roman legion and, even today, is the national symbol for at least seven countries. It is a good image for the danger described here.

Revelation uses "woe" seven times, although it is sometimes translated "alas". Stefanovic suggests they are the flip side of the seven beatitudes in Revelation. I like that. The triple use here also echoes the stark woes Jesus pronounced on the cities of Chorazin, Bethsaida and Capernaum for their unbelief, according to the Gospel of Matthew.

Cranach's angel proclaims this triple judgement over the city (Wittenberg(?)), while a personified sun, moon and stars are watching. The city looks peaceful and unaware.

I let the eagle in my painting soar over Manchester, where I live, a city with many believers but also much wickedness. I painted three "woe" angels. The gold in my painting depicts the presence of God. The altar and the fire is gone from heaven. I have resisted inserting the words, which the old illustrators found compelling to do.

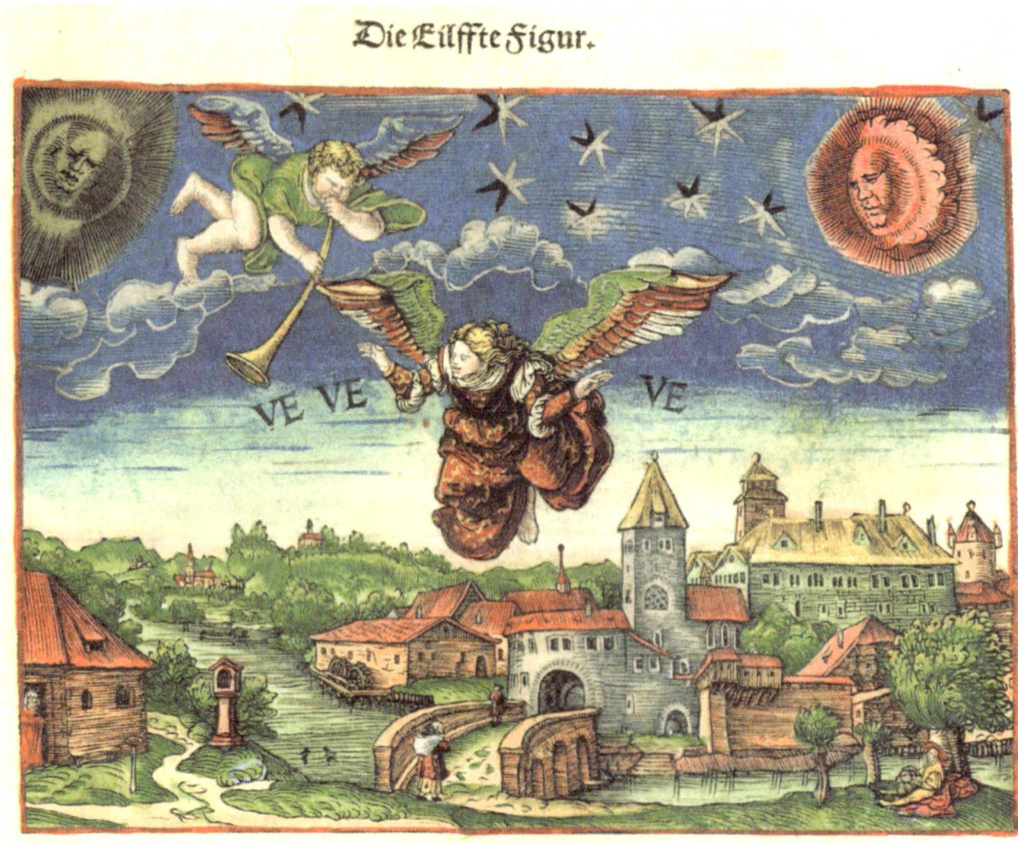

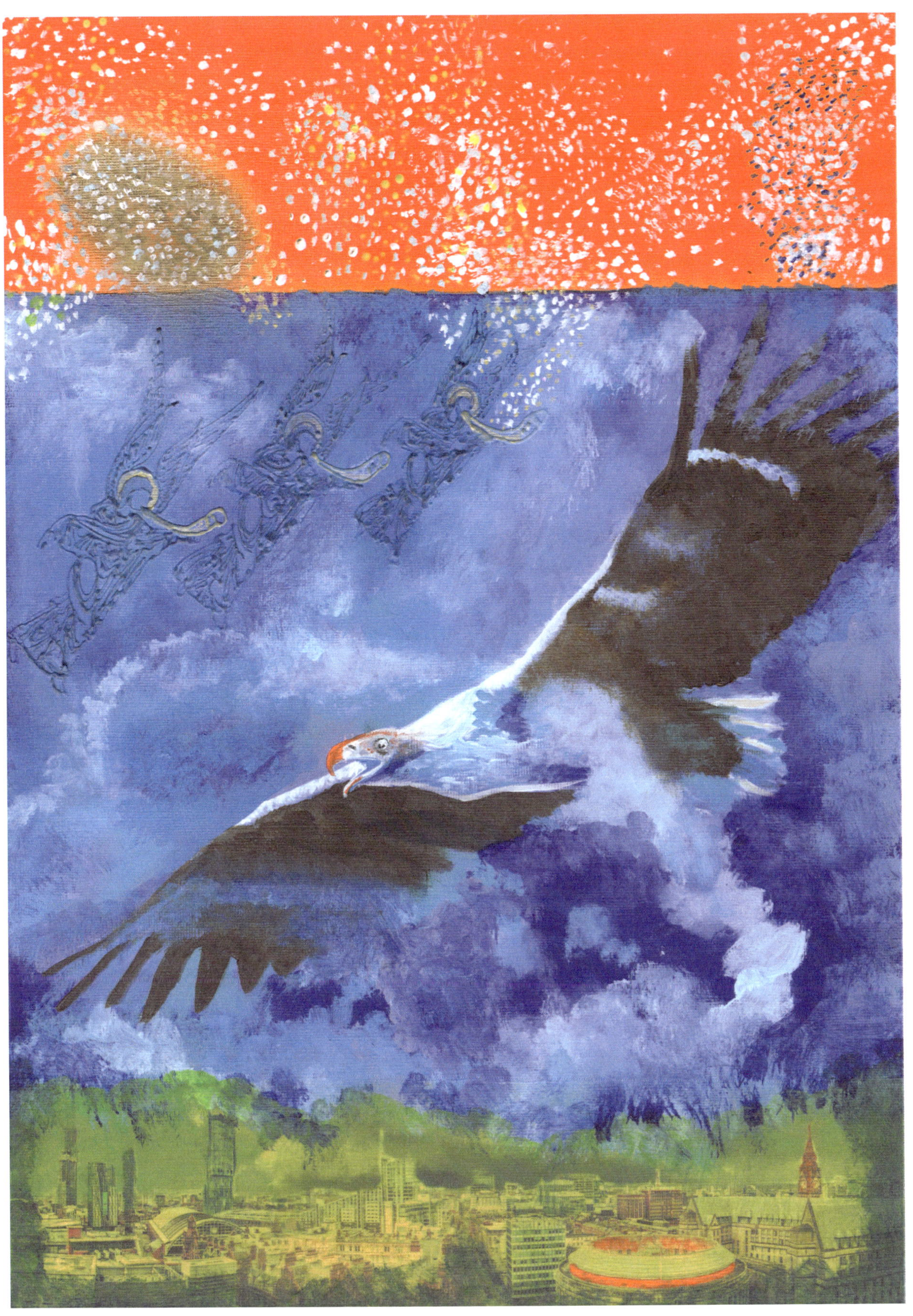

The Fifth Trumpet

This Story is about the release of demons and their demonic activity on earth, but the heart of this passage is the protection of those who have the seal of God, apparently signified by the grass and trees. Because this is what prayer does, I have painted the praying apostle John separated from the people of the earth who are being tormented. The star falling from heaven to earth is personified as he opens the "abyss". This describes a supernatural reality, which raises two further questions.

Who is the star? Commentators link it with the angel who releases Satan (Rev 20); others see Wormwood as the personification of Satan himself. I find the latter unlikely, for why would Christ give the key to Satan? This is more likely another angel doing God's bidding, receiving the key from Christ (1:18) and being told to use it.

What is the "abyss"? This word is used seven times in Revelation, always in relation to an evil place where evil creatures are imprisoned (three times in Rev 9, then in 11:7; 17:8; 20:1,3. Elsewhere it is also mentioned in Isa 24:21–22 and Luke 8:31). It refers to a physical place under the earth first mentioned in Genesis 1:2, where it unites the waters and the deep, and then in Genesis 7:11, where it is the source of the flood waters.

Ahead of the demonic powers a lot of smoke is coming out of the pit. I do not think we are dealing here with symbols representing physical armies, like the Parthians, as suggested by Keener and many other scholars. This Story focuses on the

9: [1]And the fifth angel blew his trumpet, and I saw
a star that had fallen from heaven to earth, and he
was given the key to the shaft of the bottomless pit;
[2]he opened the shaft of the bottomless pit, and from
the shaft rose smoke like the smoke of a great furnace,
and the sun and the air were darkened with the smoke
from the shaft. [3]Then from the smoke came locusts
on the earth, and they were given authority like the
authority of scorpions of the earth. [4]They were told not
to damage the grass of the earth or any green growth
or any tree, but only those people who do not have the
seal of God on their foreheads. [5]They were allowed to
torture them for five months, but not to kill them, and
their torture was like the torture of a scorpion when
it stings someone. [6]And in those days people will seek
death but will not find it; they will long to die, but
death will flee from them.

demonic and supernatural, therefore such strange, composite creatures. It is the opening of the abyss that explains why these "locusts" have the authority of "scorpions". They are not characteristic locusts, devouring vegetation; they are strange, threatening creatures [see Story Fifty-One] that torture the people who have not been sealed by God. They torture for five months, but do not kill.

Why five months? Many commentators connect the lifespan of a locust and five months. It seems odd, as these are not regular locusts. Stefanovic, in trying to work this out, makes a probable connection to the flood (Gen 7:24; 8:3). It makes some sense to me, since the waters of the abyss that were unleashed then are unleashed again in this vision, now as demonic powers.

The *Beatus*, left, depicts the pit as a pot with the Key angel above it. Smoke rises from the pot, while crude "locusts" with human faces and scorpion tails attack people (to us they look more like tortoises or frogs).

Kees de Kort, a Dutch artist who died in 2022, is one of my heroes. I remember visiting his studio and admiring his works on Amos, Job, and the Song of Songs. The "locusts" in my painting are quoted from his Amos. My Key angel is in the lower right corner. Three large scorpion tails represent the demonic dangers, often interpreted as lies, deceit, and false faith. Such a spiritual attack can only be countered by unceasing prayer (Eph 6).

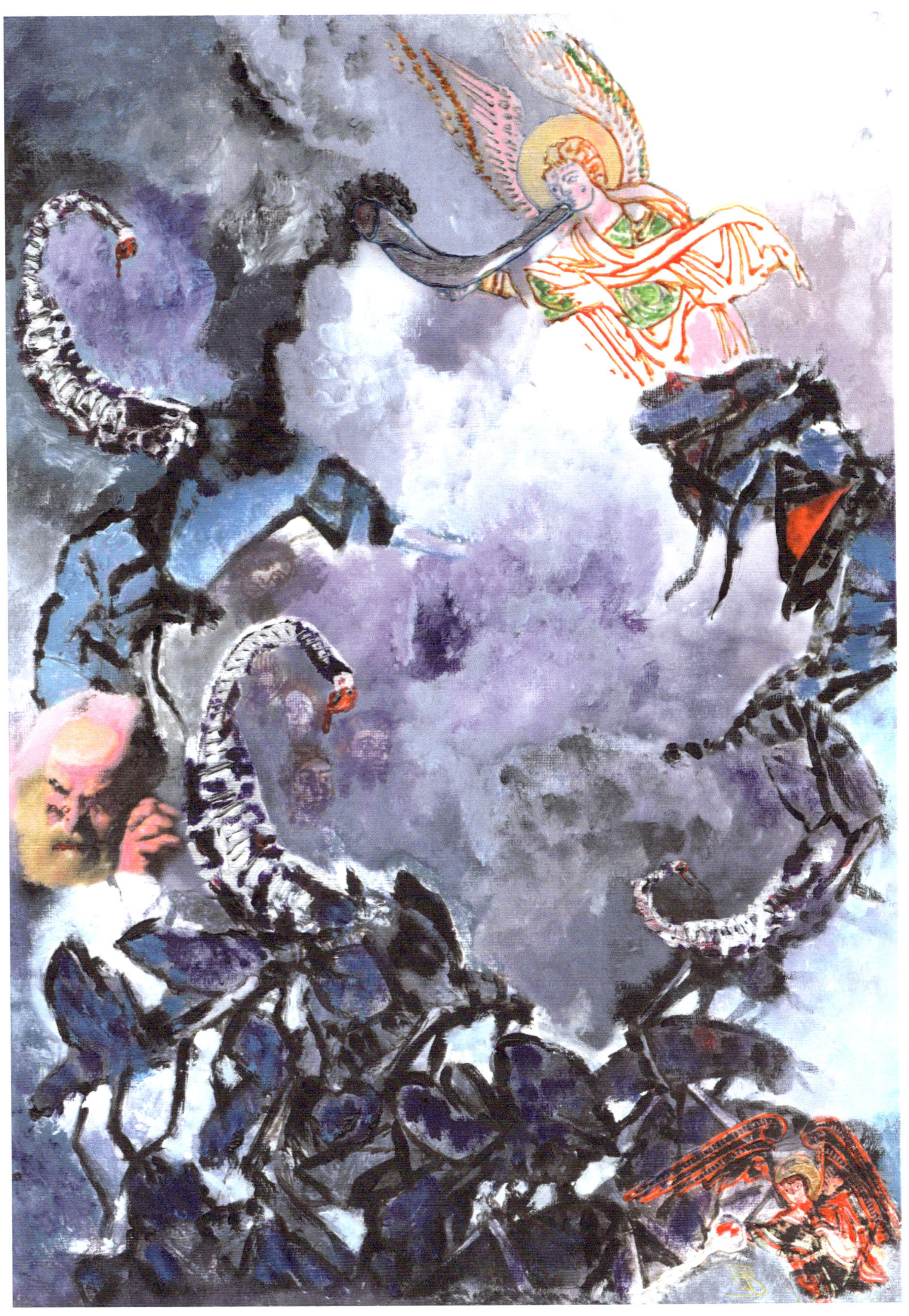

Abadditional

Joel's vision (Joel 1:2) of a locust invasion as God's judgement on Judah, as well as the locust plague in Egypt before the exodus, form the background for the action unleashed by the fifth trumpet. Some see these creatures as a curse of delusion. Leithart links it to Ezekiel 2:6 and Luke 10:18,19 and concludes it indicates the disciples will be spared the stinging words of their enemies.

It is best to see these as demonic spiritual forces that cause havoc in the spiritual, political and social realms through delusion, lies and deceit.

Who or what are the locusts? They are composite creatures and should be seen symbolically. They have limited power, because they cannot kill, only torture. Their sting is painful, like that of a scorpion. Commentators ascribe deceit and lying to the sting in the tail. These creatures appear with human faces, reminding us that evil often presents a human face. Their teeth are like lion's teeth, they have iron breastplates and make a lot of noise. The speed at which they advance and their number reminds John of war horses and chariots. They are very intimidating and instil fear, but they only do damage

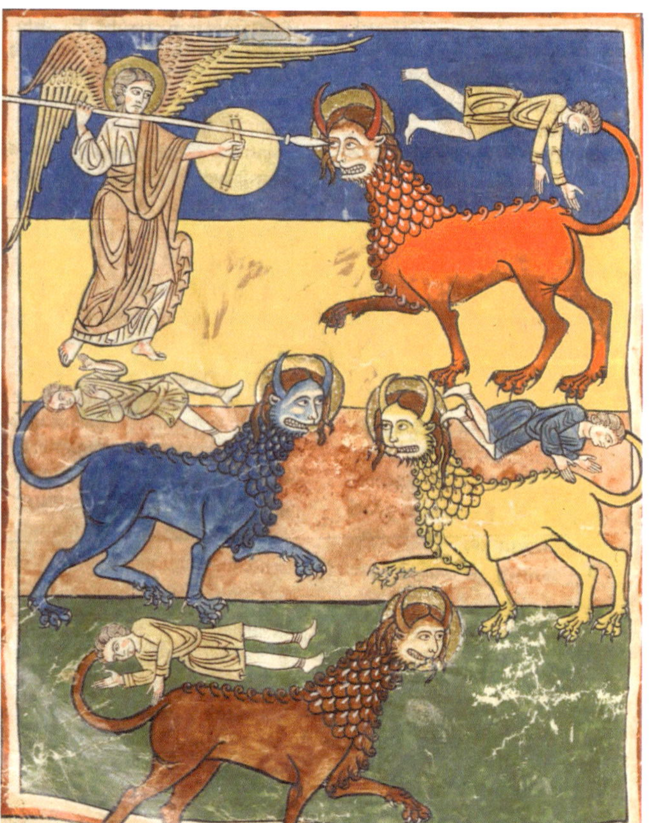

> 9: [7]*In appearance the locusts were like horses equipped for battle. On their heads were what looked like crowns of gold; their faces were like human faces,* [8]*their hair like women's hair, and their teeth like lions' teeth;* [9]*they had scales like iron breastplates, and the noise of their wings was like the noise of many chariots with horses rushing into battle.* [10]*They have tails like scorpions, with stingers, and in their tails is their power to harm people for five months.* [11]*They have as king over them the angel of the bottomless pit; his name in Hebrew is Abaddon, and in Greek he is called Apollyon.* [12]*The first woe has passed. There are still two woes to come.*

with their tails! The span of their terror is limited to "five months". In the context I doubt this refers to a literal period.

Next the locust "king" is introduced: Abaddon, or Apollyon in Greek (even though locusts do not have "kings"). The name or title means "destroyer". His task, and that of his armies, is to hurt and terrify the people of the earth [Why? will be answered soon].

I found it as hard to paint these creatures as John apparently found it to describe them, for he has to resort again and again to the words "like", "likeness". In my painting I portrayed all the attributes he describes, but not combining them into a single creature. Abaddon, seen from above, has a halo of woman's hair and a human face. The whole painting tries to express danger and disgust. I really did not enjoy making this painting and found it an oppressive struggle to imagine the evil being unveiled here.

The *Beatus* illustration has a lighter touch. The creatures look rather harmless, with only one victim "attacked" per locust looking like a horse. I like the colour scheme. Abaddon is correctly shown as an angel here, rather than one of the creatures, which is how I portrayed him in my painting.

With the first woe past, the sixth angel is now getting his trumpet ready.

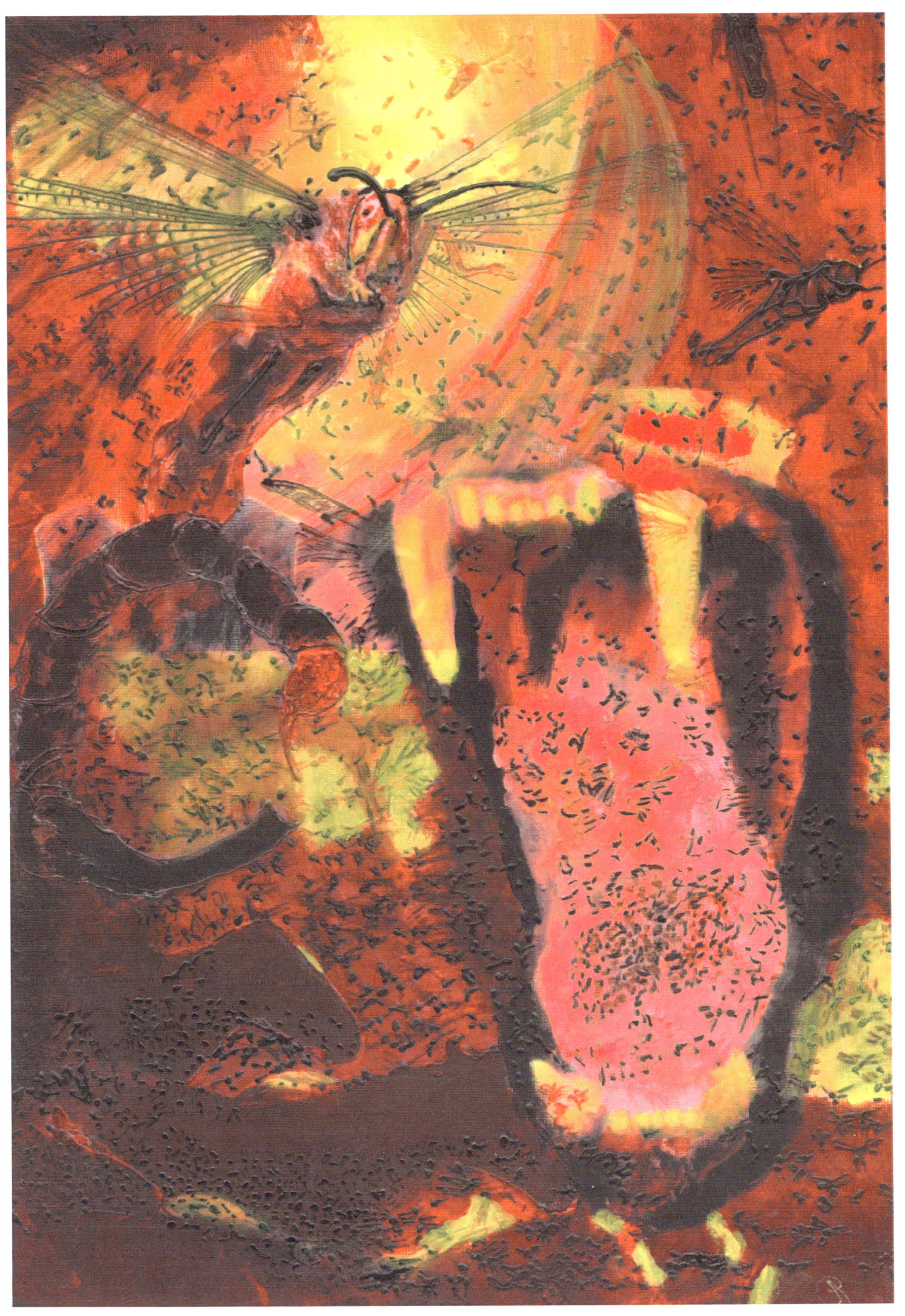

The Sixth Trumpet

The prayers of the martyrs (Rev 6) and living saints (Rev 8) are now being answered from the horned golden altar in heaven. I found it so encouraging to contemplate that angels (in this case, the Trumpet angel) are moved to action by our prayers! The *Beatus* has a lovely illustration of this scene, below. I like the varieties of fish in the river.

In my painting I show the quoted Beatus angels being unbound. Next to the angels is a pile of human bodies, representing the third of people killed, that I quote from another Amos painting by De Kort. The prayers have gone up and the voice, presumably in answer to the prayers as suggested by Swete, tells the Trumpet angel what to do. At the centre, the moon, with a suggested clock's face, indicates exact time.

Why the Euphrates? Many commentators link this vision to an attack by the Parthians in Roman times. However, we also remember that the Euphrates was the "ideal" border of Israel (as in Gen 15:18 and Exod 23:31). Everything from across the Euphrates threatened God's people, politically (most modern commentators) but also spiritually (ancient commentators). In my painting the river signifies the border against threatening spiritual hosts.

Who are these four angels? There is much debate about their identity. Many link them with the four angels of Story

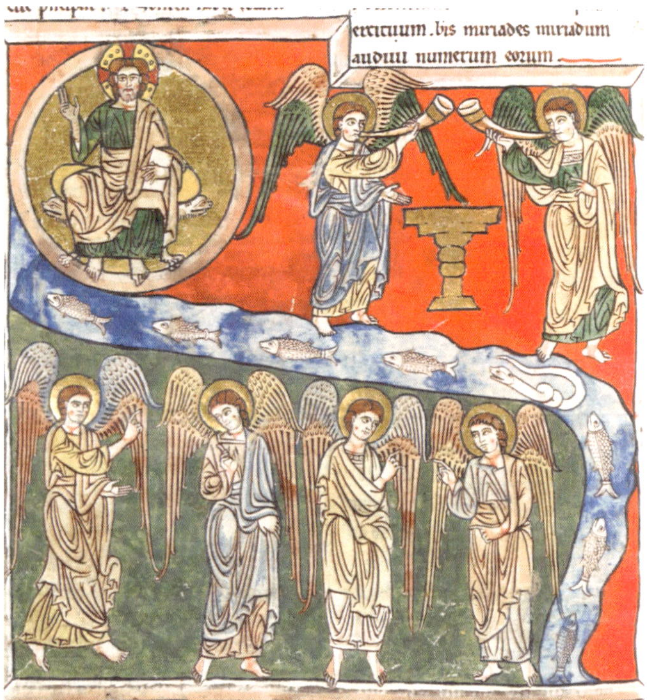

9: [13]Then the sixth angel blew his trumpet, and I heard
a voice from the four horns of the golden altar before
God, [14]saying to the sixth angel who had the trumpet,
"Release the four angels who are bound at the great
river Euphrates." [15]So the four angels were released,
who had been held ready for the hour, the day, the
month, and the year, to kill a third of humankind.

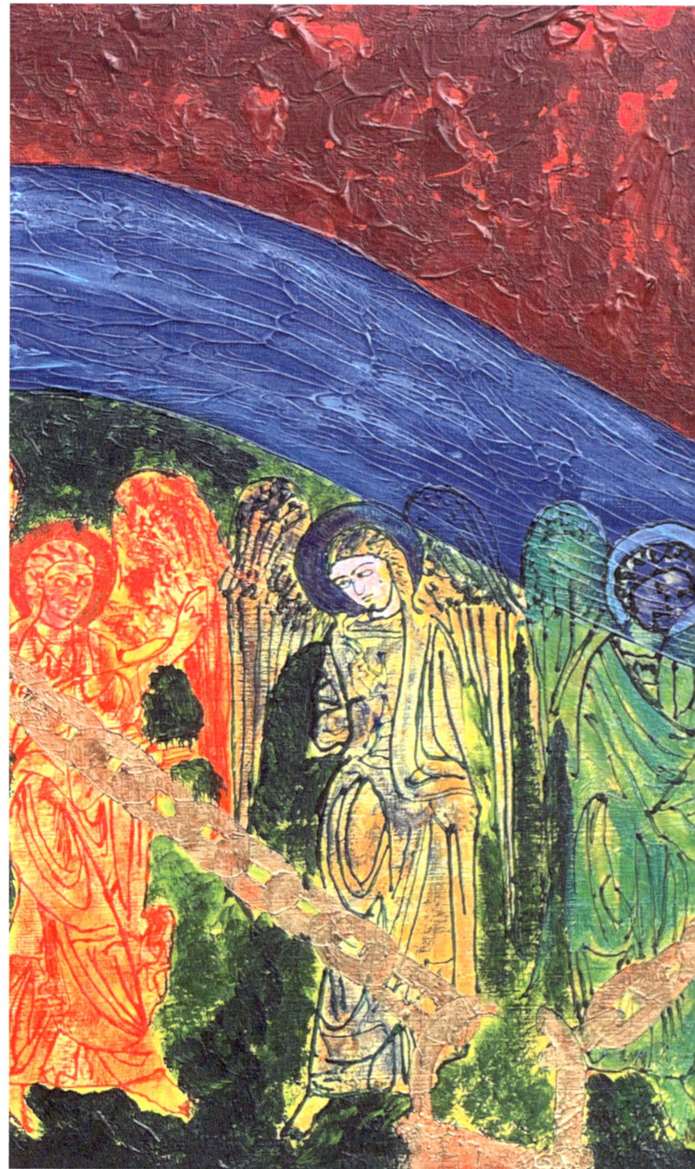

Twenty-Nine (the sixth unsealing). But they seem different. There they are holding back the winds; here they are bound and held back. Some see them as evil, others as good. I agree with those who see them as "good" angels, charged with executing God's judgement. If they were evil, I think John would have indicated that. The text does not give us any idea about how they relate to the creatures that follow ("hippo-lions", as Leithart calls them, the Greek *hippo* meaning "horse"). Greijdanus rightly draws attention to number four, interpreting it as showing the angels' activity covering the whole earth.

Why is such an apparently exact time mentioned? God set an exact time, unknown to us (Acts 1:7), in advance of it happening. It reminds us God is in perfect control. Nothing happens accidentally; "neither unplanned nor unexpected", as Ian Paul says. Jordan suggests the specific time recalls the Passover. Leithart also sees this and interprets the release of the angels as beginning a new Passover.

The angels are released to do what they "had been held ready for" by God: to kill one third of humanity. It reminds us of the angel of death who, in Egypt on the Passover night, killed the first-born who were not "sealed" by a lamb's blood. Many commentators see here merely a repeat of the evil hordes released at trumpet five.

However, I believe God does His judging through his good angels, both inside the church, to whom this letter is addressed, and outside it, on the people of the earth, God's enemies. And judgements are mysteriously linked to the prayers of the martyrs and all the living saints, also today's saints, until the day of the Lord when the final trumpet will sound.

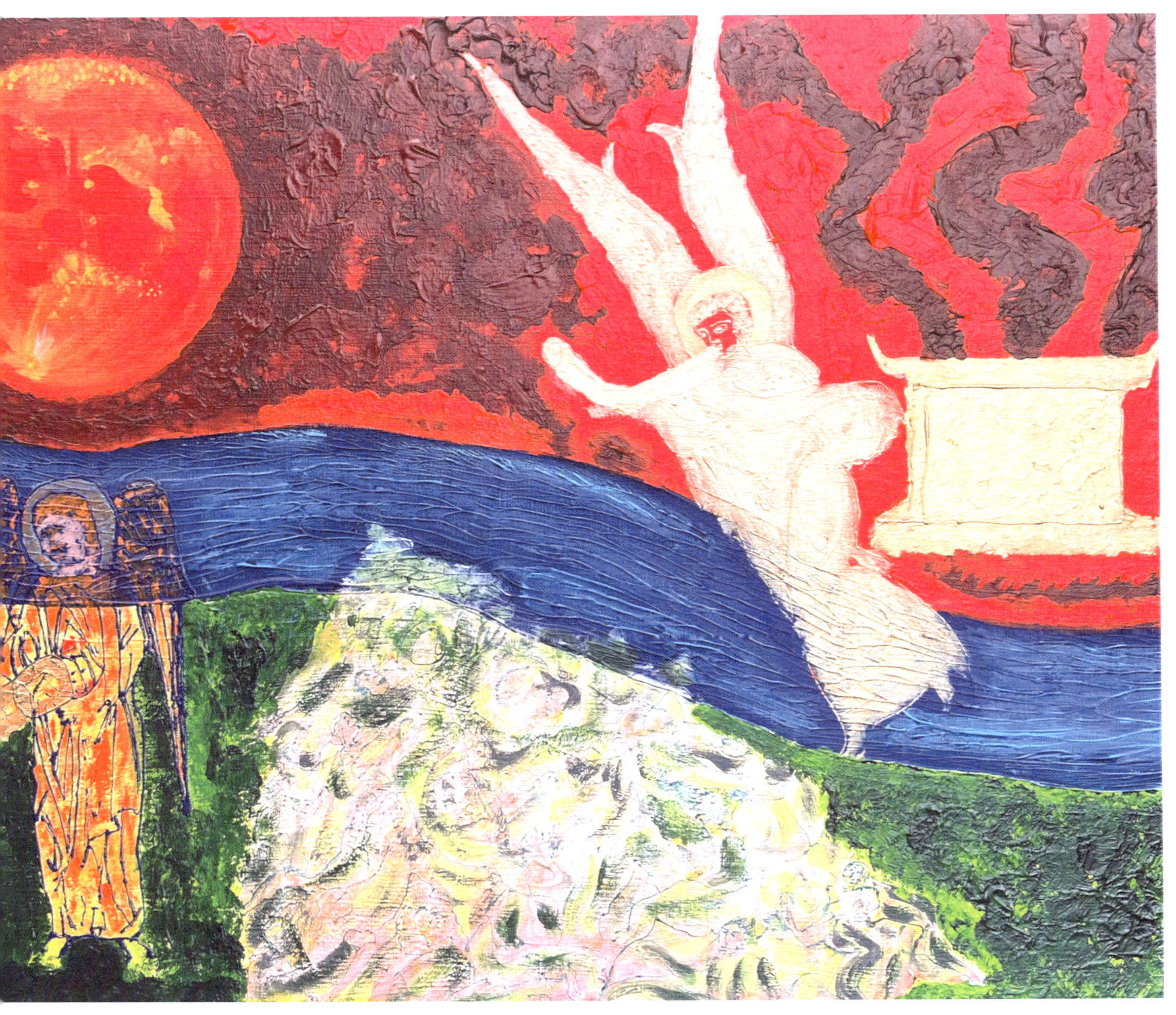

Two Myriads

When I first read this, I got very excited about painting it, even though John only heard a number. Later we see that he also saw the horsemen [Story Forty-Four], but the number intrigued me, and I had done the 144,000 before.

So how do you visualise two myriads? I had a couple of attempts, using the colours mentioned in Story Forty-Four: yellow, blue and red, representing sulphur, sapphire and fire. Things became clearer as I started to paint: first, a beautiful diamond. But then I was unsure how to turn it into what I was trying to express for this text. So I sadly discarded the first painting, shown below, for the purpose of this book, and started again...

9: [16]The number of the troops of cavalry was two hundred million; I heard their number.

It struck me that the diamond shape can also signify the shape of a "breastplate". This is useful to express my understanding that the two myriads of "hippo-lions" are most likely an army of cherubim angels (Leithart). I started painting again. As before, I divided the painting into small squares, like a 3-D grid, similar to how I painted the 144,000 in Story Thirty.

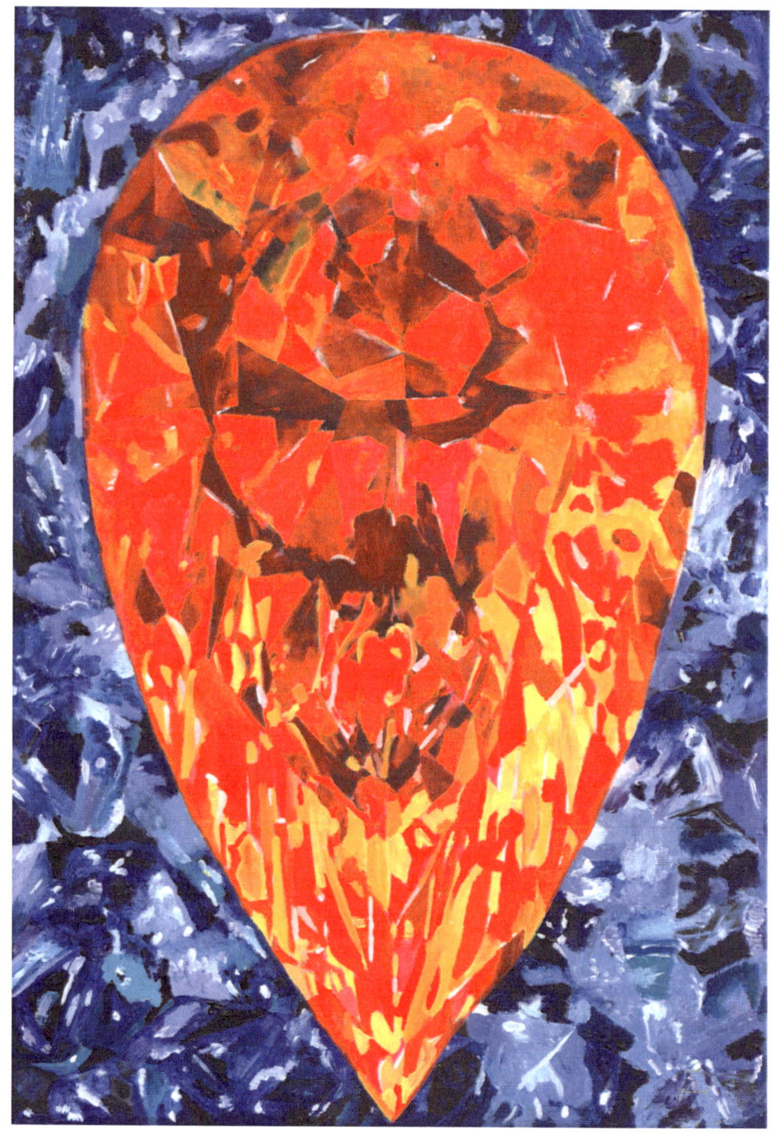

I filled all the squares with paint, but this time overran some of the edges to create a less rigid whole. Outside, in the hyacinth blue, the army of angels glitter in silver and ivory. The "dividing line" in "pure" gold separates the two myriads.

Of course, the translated text does not say "two myriads" (though the Greek word is "myriad"). Translators got out their calculators and came up with "two hundred million". In doing so, they lost something, because it is not calculation but wonder at the innumerable multitude that the text intends. One myriad is already an uncountable number; two myriads become sheer hyperbole. It is quite clear that we cannot take this number literally. Instead, it represents an army of angels that cannot be defeated: it conquers everything, leaving destruction in its wake. It is the answer to our prayers, as it was for Elisha when God opened his eyes to the armies of heaven.

Swete suggests an OT echo in Psalm 68:17: "With mighty chariotry, twice ten thousand, thousands upon thousands, the Lord came from Sinai into the holy place." Apparently, God counts that which is holy. The number here then would strengthen the case for it referring to a "holy" army.

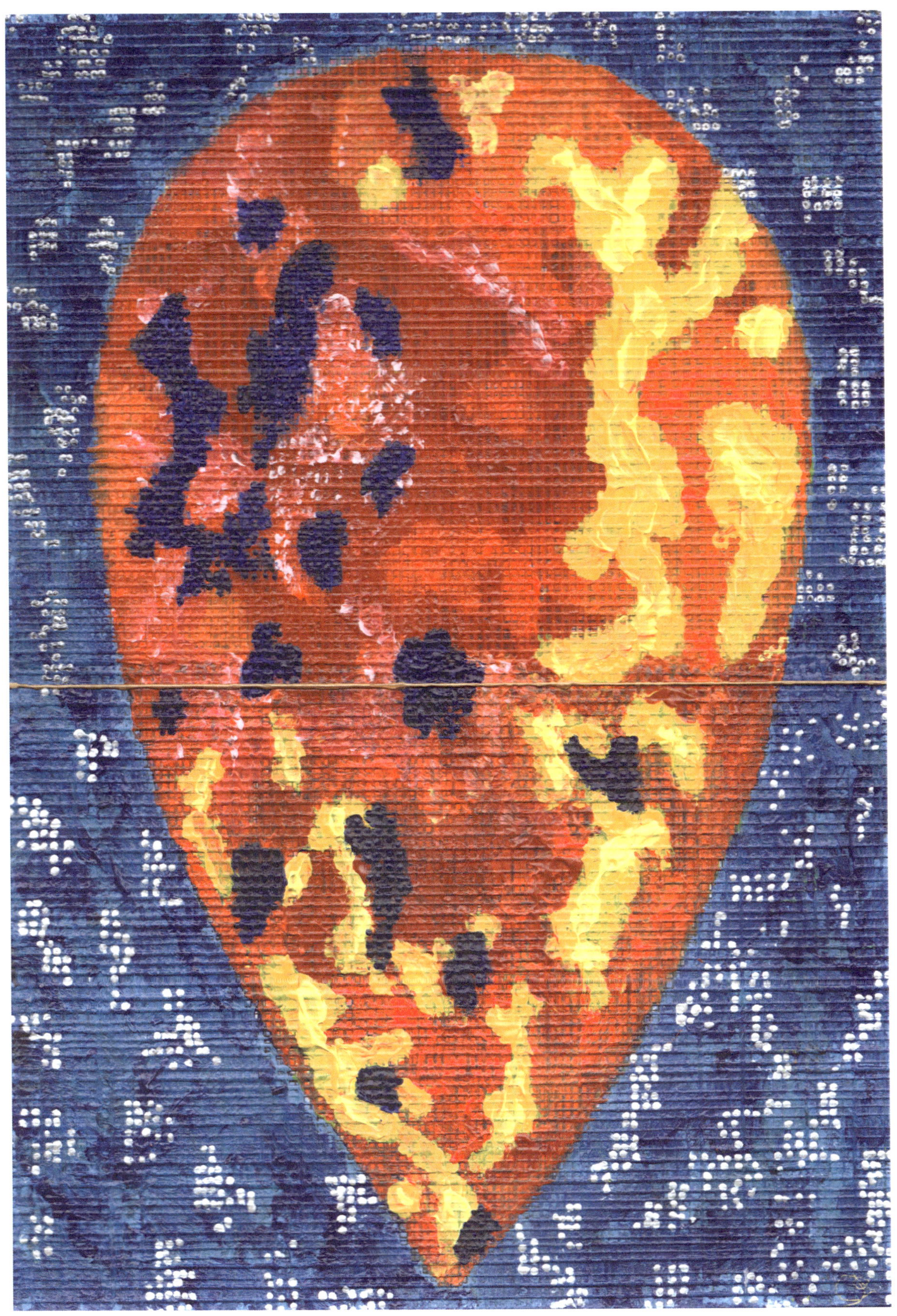

No Repentance

This army from heaven, repeated many times in my painting in the hyacinth-coloured sky, comes from behind the altar and the angel with the trumpet to bring death to a third of humanity, shown in the lower right of my painting.

I have not pictured the horsemen, for it is from the mouths of the lions' heads that the plagues proceed. I depict four creatures to show the global effect of this "woe". Their serpent-like tails cause harm, but it is the plagues from their mouths that kill.

Despite the vastness and horror of this judgement, the line of people I quote in my painting look the other way as they walk past the heads of the dead, but no one repents! [Story Forty-Five will give the reason for this callousness.]

> *9: [17]And this was how I saw the horses in my vision: the riders wore breastplates the color of fire and of sapphire and of sulfur; the heads of the horses were like lions' heads, and fire and smoke and sulfur came out of their mouths. [18]By these three plagues a third of humankind was killed, by the fire and smoke and sulfur coming out of their mouths. [19]For the power of the horses is in their mouths and in their tails; their tails are like serpents, having heads; and with them they inflict harm.[20]The rest of humankind, who were not killed by these plagues, did not repent of the works of their hands.*

The *Getty* illustration, below, shows an army with swords, on horse bodies with lion heads that breathe destruction.

But to me, these are not human armies. They are the armies of heaven bringing plague, sickness and death in an effort to judge, albeit partially, while yet offering the possibility of repentance. The judgement sadly reminds us of Pharaoh in Egypt before the first exodus, who was not moved to sincere repentance by the first nine plagues, but only after experiencing the tenth plague, in his own "flesh". And even then he only reluctantly let God's people go.

What are these "hippo-lions"? They are God's angels, cherubim-like creatures that operate in the heavenly realm, here used by God in His judgement on the powers of evil and their allies.

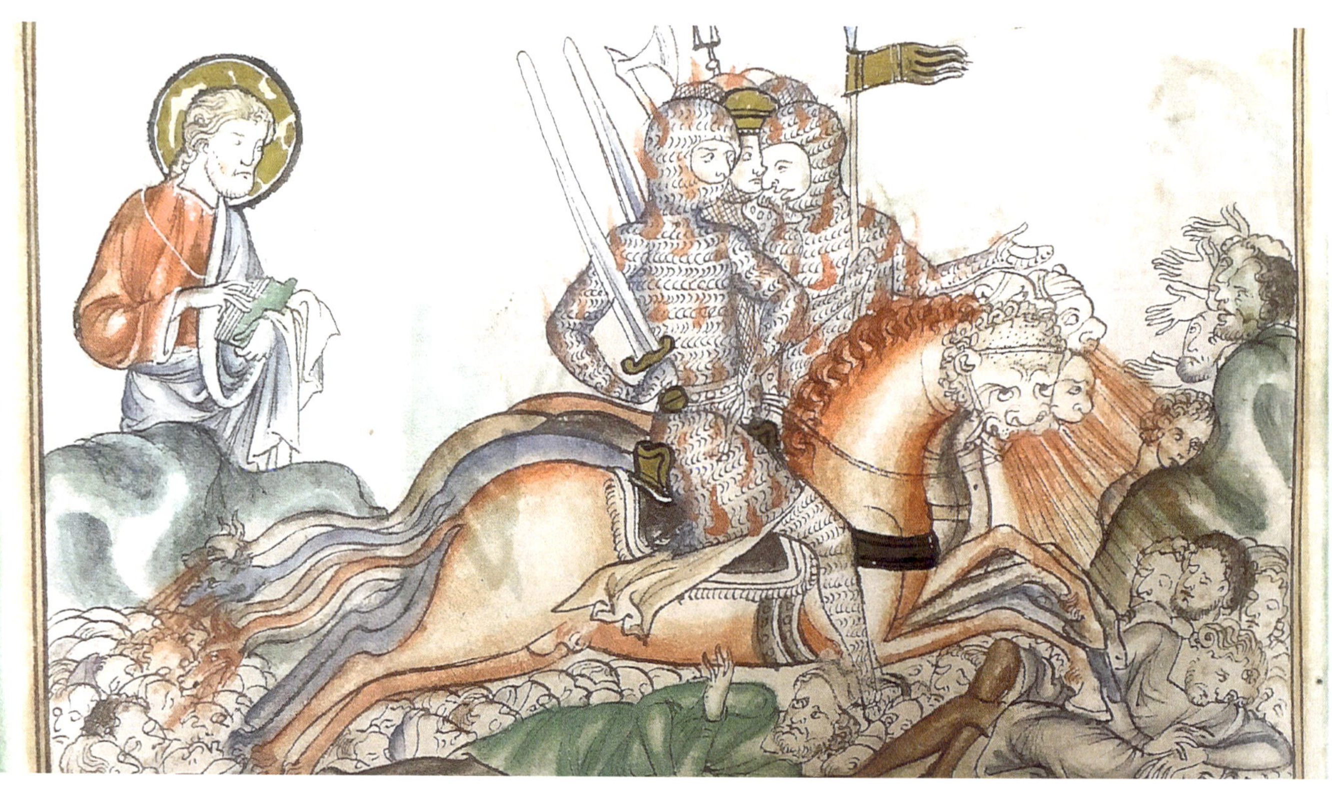

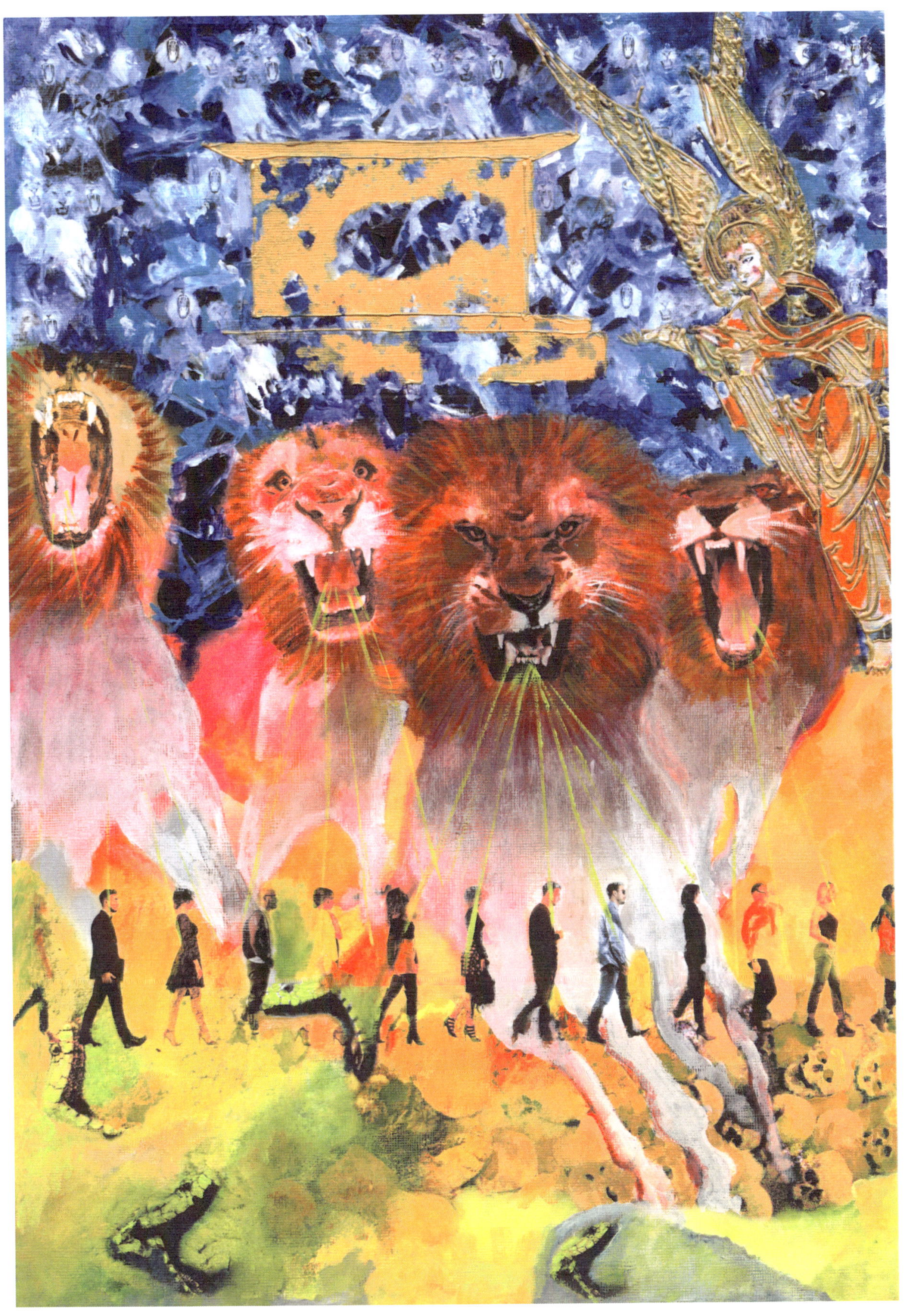

The Rest of Humanity

Despite the terrifying judgements in Story Forty-Four, John sees the people so committed to their worship of the demons and idols of gold, silver, bronze, stone and wood, which neither see nor hear nor walk, that they continue, apparently senseless, with murdering, sorceries, fornication and theft. Everything is described in sets of four, signifying the spirit of the world.

Many of us today, and many commentators, at this point want to move on quickly to what comes next. Most illuminators did not even attempt to illustrate this passage. But I decided to take time to meditate on it, and found it teaches details of what we are expected to do.

We make idols with our own hands... In my painting I show the materials for making idols in the four corners. In the centre is money (our British pound coin, symbolically representing the four countries of the United Kingdom with an English rose, a Scottish thistle, a Welsh leek and a Northern Irish shamrock, for money and the economy are at the centre of our society). For most people, money comes first. Nothing is more important than money.

Second in importance today is our "digital" presence, symbolised by a contextualised iPhone screen, through which we view our personalised world. I have painted lines of unconcerned and unrepentant people through the phone, streaming from top to bottom and from left to right, intentionally suggesting a cross, symbol of hope that can redeem this.

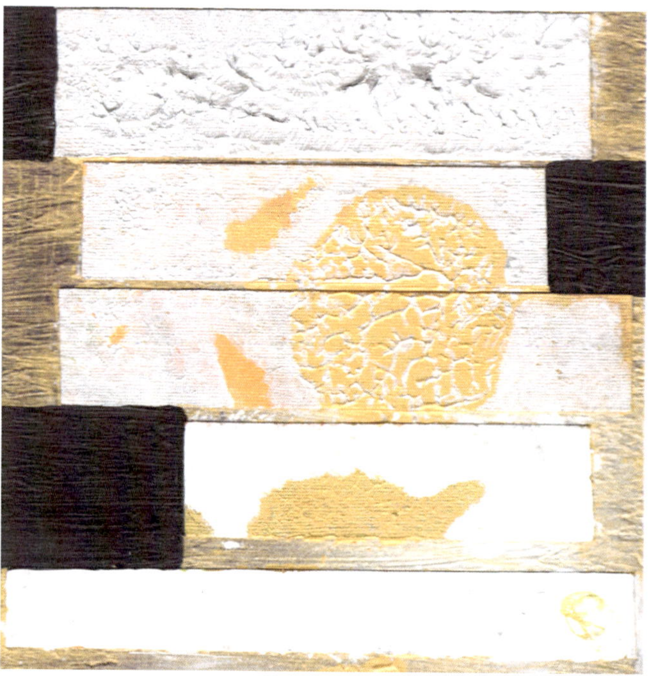

9: [20]The rest of humankind, who were not killed by these plagues, did not repent of the works of their hands or give up worshiping demons and idols of gold and silver and bronze and stone and wood, which cannot see or hear or walk. [21]And they did not repent of their murders or their sorceries or their fornication or their thefts.

Thirdly, I painted a reference to Manchester United football club (the famous trio of heroes on a pedestal at the main entrance) as example of idolatry today in our sports-crazy world. It is "oiled" by money, as people are bought and sold for their footballing skill. "Worship" is the right word for describing what happens on the terraces when the team wins!

For the fourth, I have kept more literally to the text and depicted theft, top left, cyber-theft in this case. Sorcery, which is alive and well in our world, is represented by the fortune-teller and her ball. Fornication is seen in the centre right, where a man is secretly kissing another woman while holding his wife. A murder has been committed in the lower right corner.

We sometimes forget that we still have the "old" idols around us too. The Hindu goddess depicted here represents them. It could have been quoted from any number of worship places in and around Manchester, where I live, or the rest of the world.

The great deceiver Abaddon, released at the sound of the fifth trumpet, is included to the left, just above the centre. His lies having achieved their purpose, his followers are focused on what he next sets before them.

Finally, apparently conducting it all, I quote an imagined health-and-wealth worshipper who embodies individualism and the worship of money, technology and false gods of our own making.

This painting is a harsh critique on our socio-economic systems, our churches and spirituality. Like the seven churches, we need the help of the seven eyes of God to see through the deceit of our age and respond in repentance.

We expect the seventh trumpet next, but before that the second woe has more to reveal...

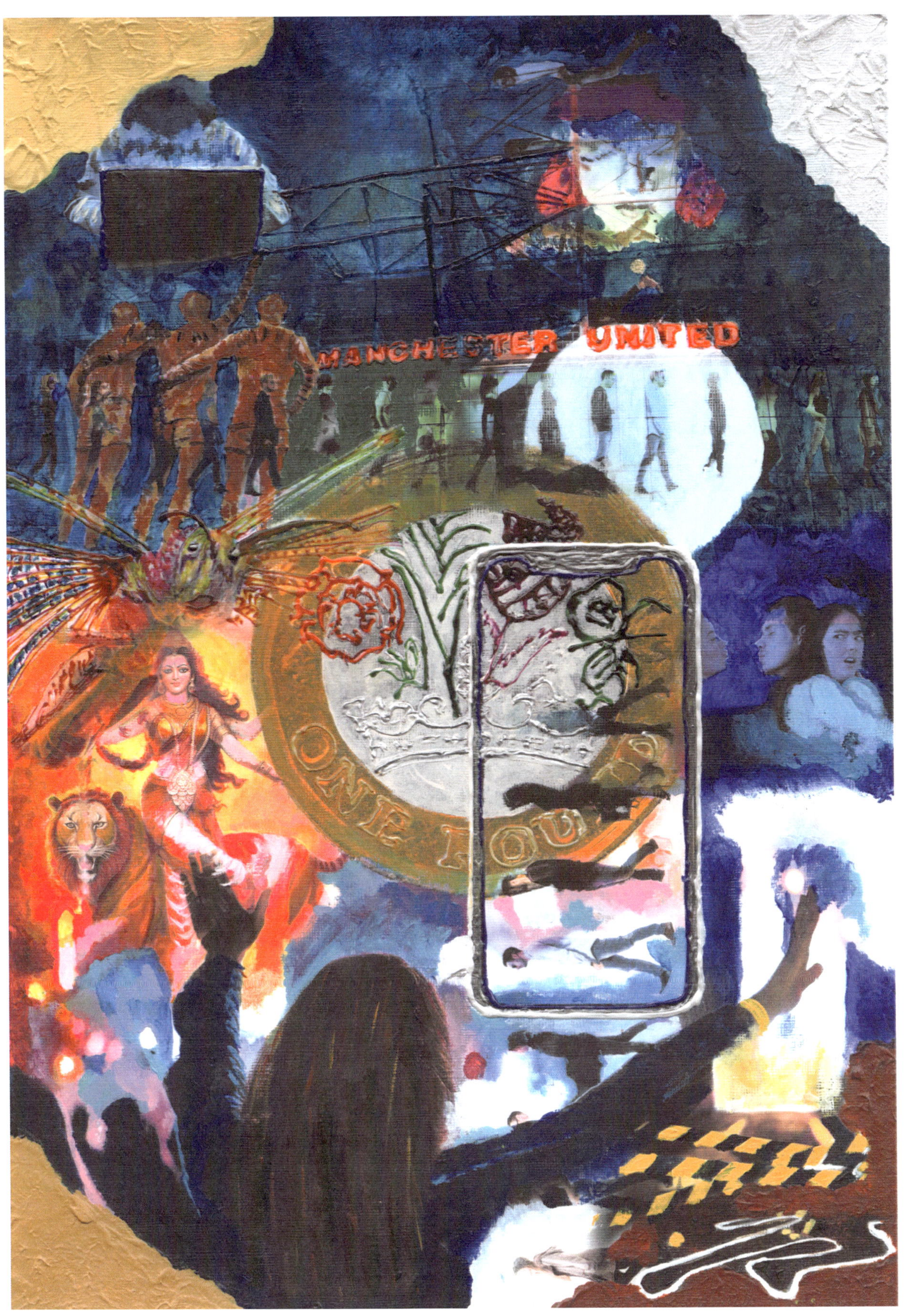
MANCHESTER UNITED

The Other Mighty Angel

The sixth trumpet now causes what many call an "interlude". It seems to me that the break is in direct response to the people of the earth who are unwilling to repent, despite the signs of the terrors of hell and the armies of heaven. At this point, John sees another powerful angel (the first one came in Story Twenty).

I have quoted the image in my painting from Anneke Kaai, whose work (below) comments on the whole of Revelation 10. I find hers an inspiring painting and admire it very much, although a little too dark... I responded by including a lot of colour and light. I quote the sea and the earth from my paintings at Story Thirty-Five and Thirty-Six. And used the trumpets to indicate the sound of seven thunders. One hand makes an oath; the other holds the open scroll.

Who is this angel? Clouds, rainbow, face like a sun, pillars of fire all remind us of the vision of Jesus in Revelation 1. Many commentators conclude that this is another vision of Jesus. But John calls him an "angel". And Jesus is never referred to as an angel. It is clear that there is a close relationship between this angel and Jesus, and I agree with those who have gone back to the opening verses of Revelation 1 and identify him as possibly the Revealing angel of the Lord.

The gigantic size of the angel, who connects heaven with sea and sky, should prepare us for a message that concerns the whole of creation. In his hand he has an open scroll.

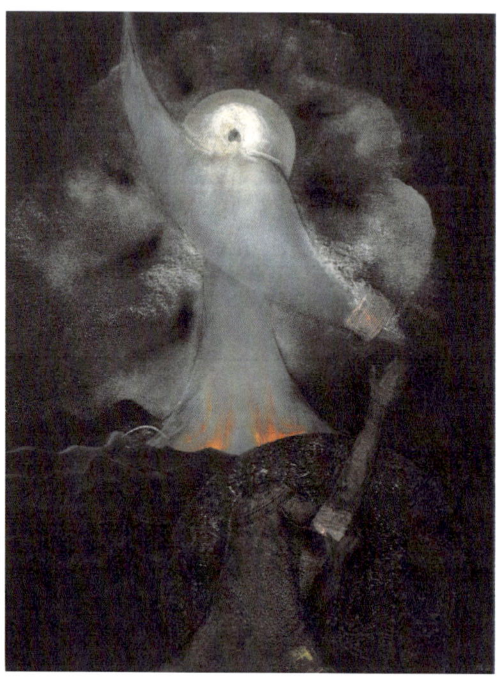

*10: 1And I saw another mighty angel coming down
from heaven, wrapped in a cloud, with a rainbow over
his head; his face was like the sun, and his legs like
pillars of fire. 2He held a little scroll open in his hand.
Setting his right foot on the sea and his left foot on the
land, 3he gave a great shout, like a lion roaring. And
when he shouted, the seven thunders sounded. 4And
when the seven thunders had sounded, I was about to
write, but I heard a voice from heaven saying, "Seal up
what the seven thunders have said, and do not write it
down." 5Then the angel whom I saw standing on the
sea and the land raised his right hand to heaven 6and
swore by him who lives forever and ever, who created
heaven and what is in it, the earth and what is in it,
and the sea and what is in it: "There will be no more
delay, 7but in the days when the seventh angel is to
blow his trumpet, the mystery of God will be fulfilled,
as he announced to his servants the prophets."*

What is this small scroll? I agree with Bauckham, and many others, that this scroll is identical to the sealed scroll of Revelation 5, which is now presented to us as an open book. The diminutive size may be to allow it to be eaten. The point is: this is an open, unsealed scroll. [We will explain more in Story Forty-Seven.]

What is this mystery that is fulfilled or finished? In my opinion it most likely refers to the last mystery, to be revealed in Revelation 22, namely the mystery of the marriage between Christ and His bride (Eph 5:32). Commentators also refer to the mystery of the inclusion of the Gentiles, which is the gospel mystery of Christ's life and work. Both of these can be included, but most important is the ultimate unity of Christ and His church.

Much ink has been spent on the thunders. John was asked not to reveal what the thunders said, but many commentators do not hesitate to suggest what they said, some claiming to know! The truth is, we do not know, and may never know.

What I find significant here is how John (assuming God expected more of the same from him) immediately prepares to write what he sees and hears. Many modern commentators do not believe this. They assume the text was written up at a very different time from seeing the vision. But God apparently stopped John from writing, instructing him to "seal up" what he had already written down and turn his attention, instead, to the unsealed, open book.

Now there is no more delay [which I picture on the next page] as Story Forty-Six runs seamlessly into Story Forty-Seven.

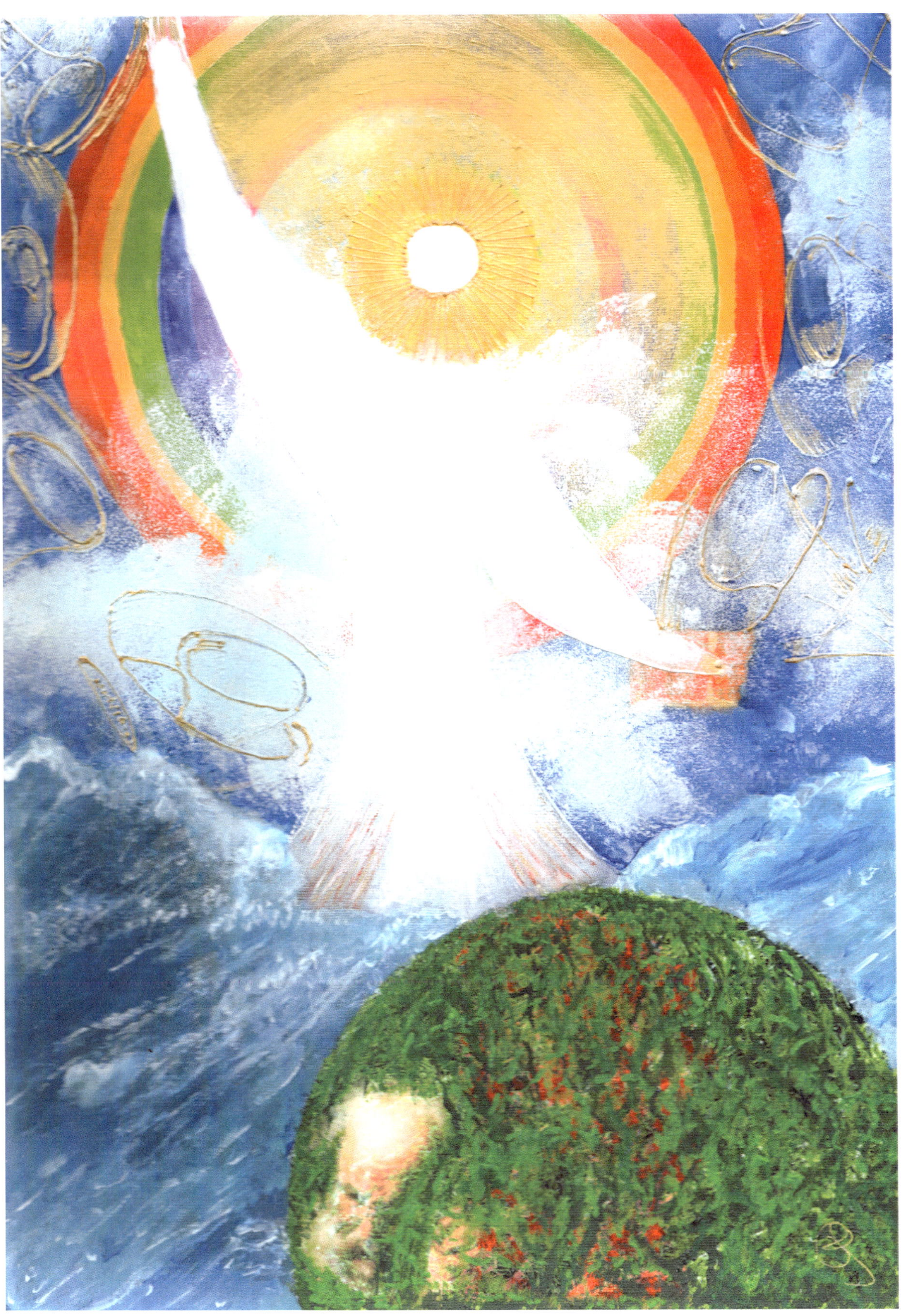

Sweet and Bitter

We ended Story Forty-Six with "there will be no more delay." The text actually says there will be no more "time". When the seventh angel blows his trumpet, time is finished. In context, this probably means that the time for repentance is over. It is not an ultimate statement about the end of earthly time.

In my painting I have depicted this as time literally "running out" in the hourglass. The Mighty angel is about to give the book to John to eat: black is the colour of bitterness, and the honeycomb refers to sweetness. The hand with the scroll and John are quoted from my painting in Story Twenty, to make the connection that this is the same scroll.

Dürer's woodcut, below, concentrates on John's devouring the book, and this illustration also covers the whole of Revelation 10, including helpfully connecting with the altar in heaven, not just the sky.

10: [8]Then the voice that I had heard from heaven spoke to me again, saying, "Go, take the scroll that is open in the hand of the angel who is standing on the sea and on the land." [9]So I went to the angel and told him to give me the little scroll; and he said to me, "Take it, and eat; it will be bitter to your stomach, but sweet as honey in your mouth." [10]So I took the little scroll from the hand of the angel and ate it; it was sweet as honey in my mouth, but when I had eaten it, my stomach was made bitter. [11]Then they said to me, "You must prophesy again about many peoples and nations and languages and kings."

Why now? That is the question I asked myself as I read this. Why is John only now being initiated as a prophet? For both Ezekiel (Ezek 1–3) and Jeremiah (Jer 1) this happened at the start of their prophetic career. One commentator suggests that this passage belongs chronologically at the beginning of Revelation, but I interpret it as John being enabled to prophesy only when the scroll is open, as it is here. In Revelation 1, John was called to be God's scribe. At this point, he "graduates" from scribe to prophet. But prophecy requires more than transcribing.

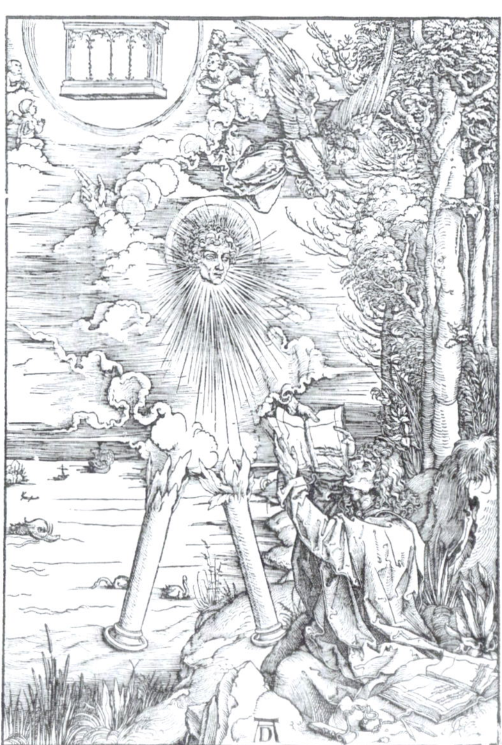

"Take and eat" reminds us of the Eucharist, although most commentators see no connection. In the Eucharist we are reminded of and comforted in the bitter sweetness of "Christ in us" and of his gospel that we proclaim.

What is in the scroll? Clearly it is a book that contains the revelation of God. With Ezekiel and Jeremiah, there was no indication about the contents of the book they had to eat. Here commentators are quick to offer suggestions. Some say it is the Bible; others, the gospel; still others select 11:1–15 or Revelation 12–22. It is probably a combination of the last two, but I also think it may be obscure on purpose.

What is the content of the scroll? It seems to me John is asked to extend his scope, from the seven churches to the peoples, nations, languages and kings of the world. At least, it intensifies and updates his calling, with Revelation 11 to the end of the Apocalypse as what was next revealed to him. And through him, now to us, that we may in turn proclaim it to the world in our time. [It will include the final judgement of all the powers and Babylon, and the establishment of God's eternal kingdom in his new creation, where Christ and His church are one.]

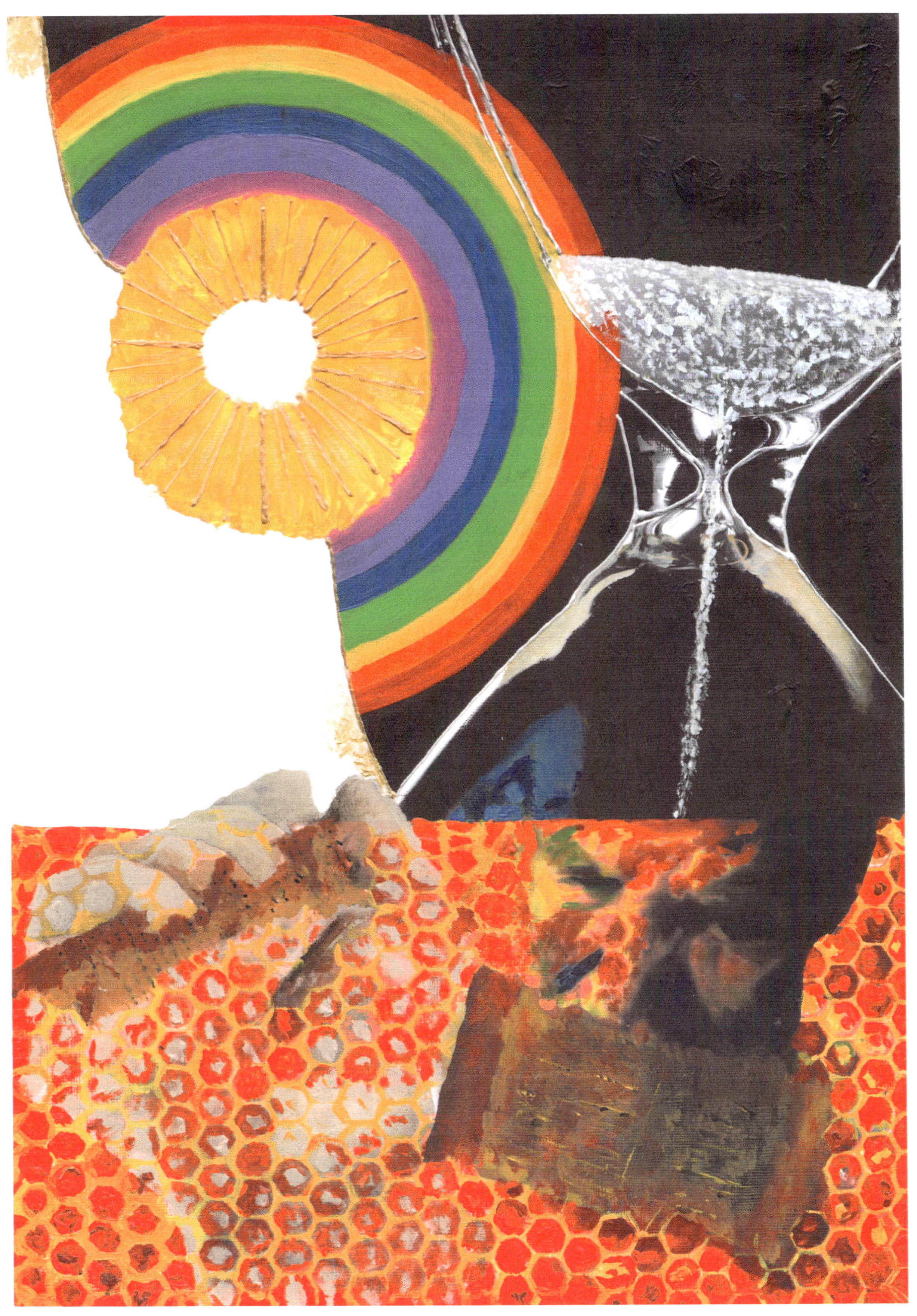

Measuring the Temple

In this Story, things are happening in heaven and on earth. John is immediately set to work on his new prophetic task. As in the days of Ezekiel and Daniel, what happens in heaven has repercussions on earth.

John is given an authoritative reed (like a "staff") as measuring rod and instructed to measure, but no actual measuring is recorded as taking place. There is some debate about this. On balance, I think that the temple of God and the altar here can only describe the heavenly temple and altar. This task looks forward prophetically to the measuring of the heavenly temple in Revelation 22, where actual measuring will take place but by an angel. The Greek word translated as "temple" is "inner sanctuary".

I agree with those commentators who see here the open scroll being enacted for the first time. The measuring then sets the tone for the whole of Revelation 11, which in turn is a kind of introduction to all that will happen next.

Why measuring? It is a symbolic and prophetic act. In the OT, measuring can symbolise ownership, preservation and/or destruction. It can also separate sacred from profane (Ezek 40–48 and 2 Sam 8:2). In the context here it most likely indicates preservation, in preparation for the seventh trumpet (Ezek 8–9 shows that the inner sanctuary in heaven is unassailable).

John seems to be using a literary pattern that has been noted by many commentators. The span of 42 months in 11:2 recurs in 13:1–10 as a time of oppression; 1260 days (=42 months or

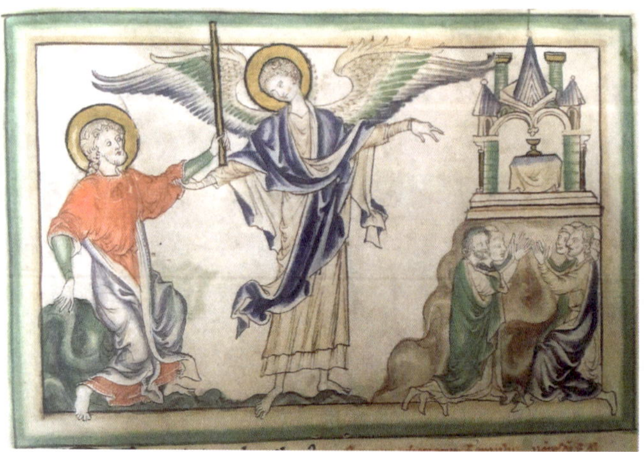

11: [1]Then I was given a measuring rod like a staff, and I was told, "Come and measure the temple of God and the altar and those who worship there, [2]but do not measure the court outside the temple; leave that out, for it is given over to the nations, and they will trample over the holy city for forty-two months."

three and a half years) in 11:3 and 12:6 is a time of preservation; 11:2–3 identify a time when the nations are threatening, yet God's witnesses are active. For John's readers, both aspects characterise the time in which they live (Resseguie). And I would suggest it is ever so in these last days.

Measuring also has other layers of meaning. It reminds us of the act of sealing in Revelation 7 to identify and protect the people of God. When the people of God are identified as the temple of God in the NT, it may point to 3:12, where they are identified as "pillars" in God's temple.

What will not be measured? The outer court, also in heaven, is left out. Perhaps because it may become the battleground in Michael's war against Satan? This war has repercussions in heaven and on earth.

According to Smalley, the temple of God here can symbolise the holy, sealed people of God; likewise the "outer court" can symbolise the church in its subjection to the powers of evil. Or, the temple can represent the church, and the outer court refers perhaps to the rejected synagogue, as in 2:9 and 3:9?

In my painting I show the measuring taking place in heaven, of the new Jerusalem (=the church, the people of God) and the golden altar. The enthroned one and the Lamb look on, but outside what's being measured, people continue to ignore God, including the (partial) "synagogue of Satan" (Rev 2).

Measuring speaks of heavenly security and earthly perseverance for those who are measured and sealed, but for those who do not believe it finalises judgement; the time of repentance is drawing to an end.

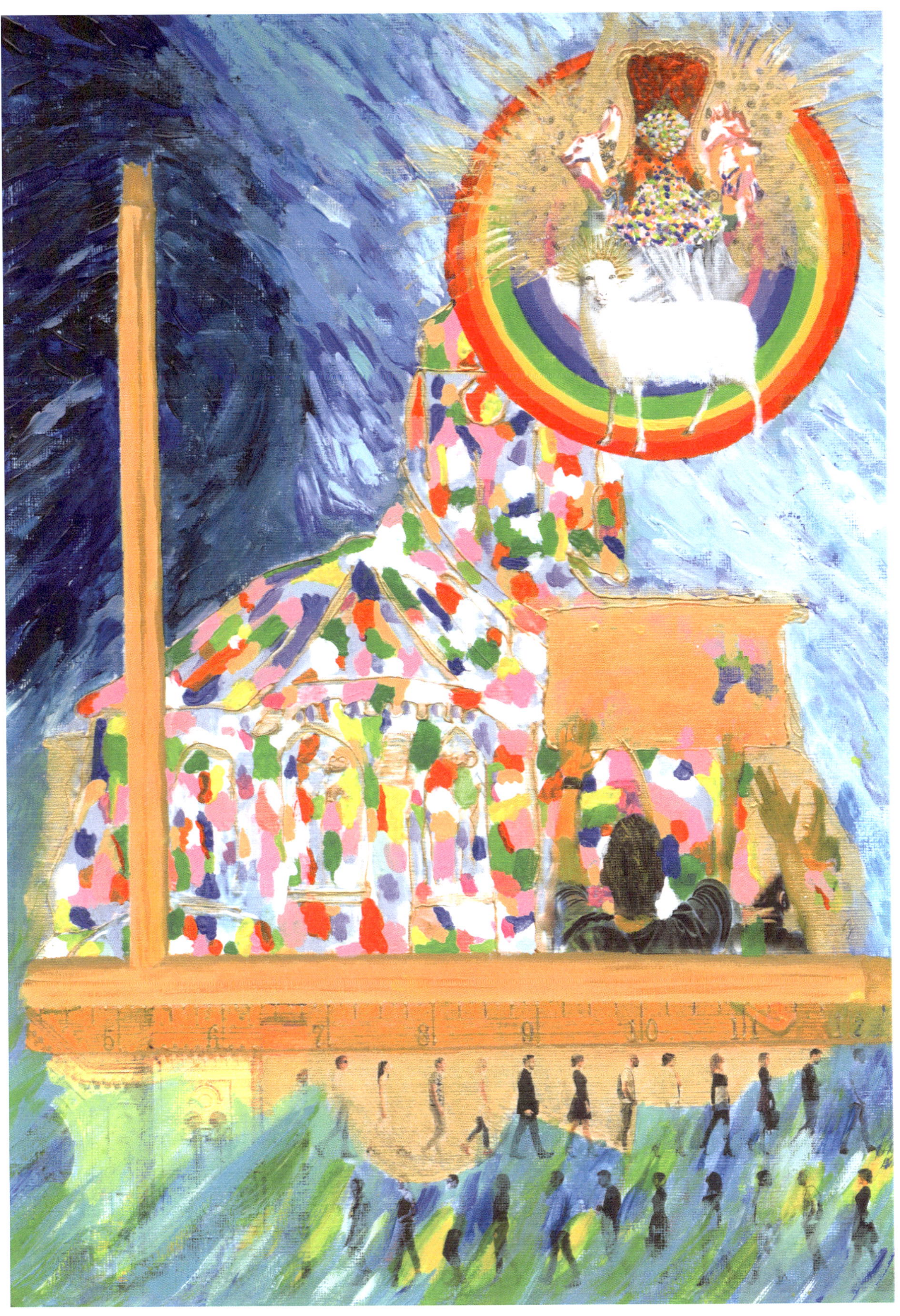
5
6
7
8
9
10
11
12

"My Two Witnesses"

Who are the two witnesses? There has been a lot of suggestions for who these two are. The church fathers suggested Moses and Elijah, or in one case, Moses and Jeremiah. And one can see why, for these witnesses are of the same calibre, doing the same kind of miracles. Others suggest they stand for the Law and the Prophets, or for the Law and the Gospel. The Old and New Testaments have also been proposed; and some suggest Peter and Paul, as they see this passage mainly dealing with apostolic times. Ellul suggests the two witnesses refer to Jesus Himself, as Son of God and Son of Man. Even others suggest they are symbols for the whole church being kings and priests. Or that they refer to two particular congregations. And so on...

How do you make up your mind in a case like this? Firstly, these two witnesses are described as "my" prophets: God's prophets. The witnesses are further called two olive trees and two lampstands, echoing Zechariah 4. But the repeated "two" here indicates the legal and spiritual authority of their testimony.

Secondly, they are dressed in sackcloth, a symbol for mourning and penitence (Matt 11:22).

Thirdly, they are given power, shown by fire from the mouth (reminiscent of the sword that comes out of the mouth of the Son of Man in Story Six?), symbolising the judgement of God that kills those who harm the witnesses. The witnesses are given power to perform signs, like Elijah and Moses, including to initiate plagues.

11: [3]"And I will grant my two witnesses authority to prophesy for one thousand two hundred sixty days, wearing sackcloth." [4]These are the two olive trees and the two lampstands that stand before the Lord of the earth. [5]And if anyone wants to harm them, fire pours from their mouth and consumes their foes; anyone who wants to harm them must be killed in this manner. [6]They have authority to shut the sky, so that no rain may fall during the days of their prophesying, and they have authority over the waters to turn them into blood, and to strike the earth with every kind of plague, as often as they desire.

The literary parallelism in the Greek between the time specified for "I will give to my two witnesses" in 11:3 and the time "it was given over to the nations" in 11:2, according to Sweet, connects the courtyard being trampled, which God allows, and the commissioning of the witnesses as "two sides of the same coin". And the time span links these with the period of the beast in Revelation 13 and 14. So Revelation 11 functions as introduction to what follows.

In the *Getty* below we see Elijah and Enoch identified as the fire-spitting witnesses. Some of their audience hear and live; others die.

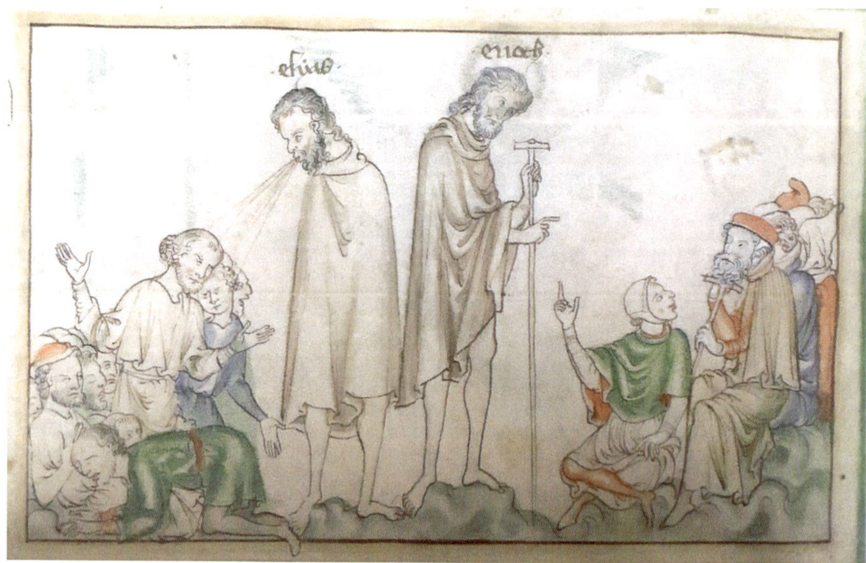

In my painting I have painted Peter and Paul, in sackcloth, as representative and "foundation" of the church (one an apostle to Jews; the other, to Gentiles). I connected them by two lampstands and two churches (quoted from Story Eight). The dark blue at the top represents a rainless sky; and the red at the bottom, the waters turning to blood.

It seems to me that such diverse interpretations can be accommodated, as long as one leaves a possibility that it can also refer to two actual witnesses, still to appear before the final day, including taking these two witnesses as the testimony of the church in the period from Christ's ascension to the future Parousia (i.e. Osborne).

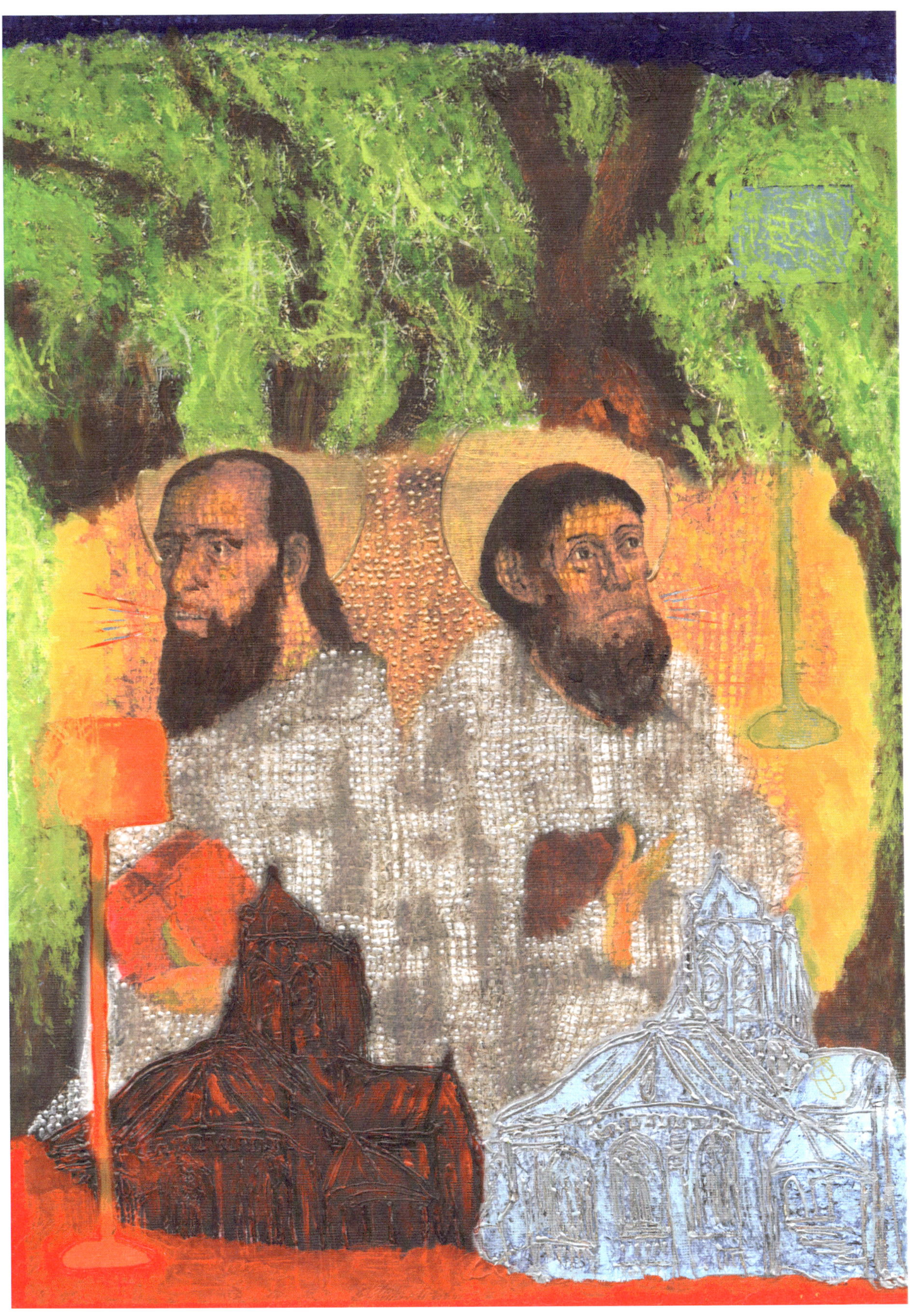

Witnesses conquered by the Beast

Only after the witnesses have finished their testimony they are killed, martyred by the beast who "makes war" on them. Some commentators take this as proof that the two witnesses refer to a group, as it would be unusual to declare war on two individuals.

Who is this beast? I will not discuss the beast here as it will take centre stage in my next volume. At this point we read that the beast comes from the bottomless pit, so it may be Abaddon, whom we met in Story Forty-One. Others identify it as the beast from the Sea in Revelation 13. The illustration from *Luther* below makes no attempt to link the beast to either of the above-mentioned. But it is adorned with a papal tiara, leaving no doubt as to how Luther interpreted the nature of this beast.

11: [7]When they have finished their testimony, the beast that comes up from the bottomless pit will make war on them and conquer them and kill them, [8]and their dead bodies will lie in the street of the great city that is prophetically called Sodom and Egypt, where also their Lord was crucified. [9]For three and a half days members of the peoples and tribes and languages and nations will gaze at their dead bodies and refuse to let them be placed in a tomb; [10]and the inhabitants of the earth will gloat over them and celebrate and exchange presents, because these two prophets had been a torment to the inhabitants of the earth.

What city is this? It pictures, above all, Jerusalem as Sodom and Egypt. In my own painting I depict Times Square, and New York as the great city representing all the cities of the world, including "Jerusalem", "Babylon" and "Rome"...

I painted the two witnesses as skeletons to show that they really died, having been destroyed by the beast (with ten horns, as I identify it as the beast from the Sea from the literary connection mentioned in Story Forty-Nine). However, I painted only one head, as it is not yet fully revealed. [We will get the full picture in Book four.]

The death of the witnesses may lead us closer to their identity. The description here makes a strong connection with Jesus, who ministered for three and a half years and was raised from death on the third day. The reference to His crucifixion reinforces this. But the two witnesses also represent His church in their witness for Him and to Him, both then, now and into the future. That would imply that the church appears to die. And the world appears to have triumphed, with the people of the earth celebrating.

But, just as the death of Jesus on the cross was not His end, so the death of the witnesses is not their end...

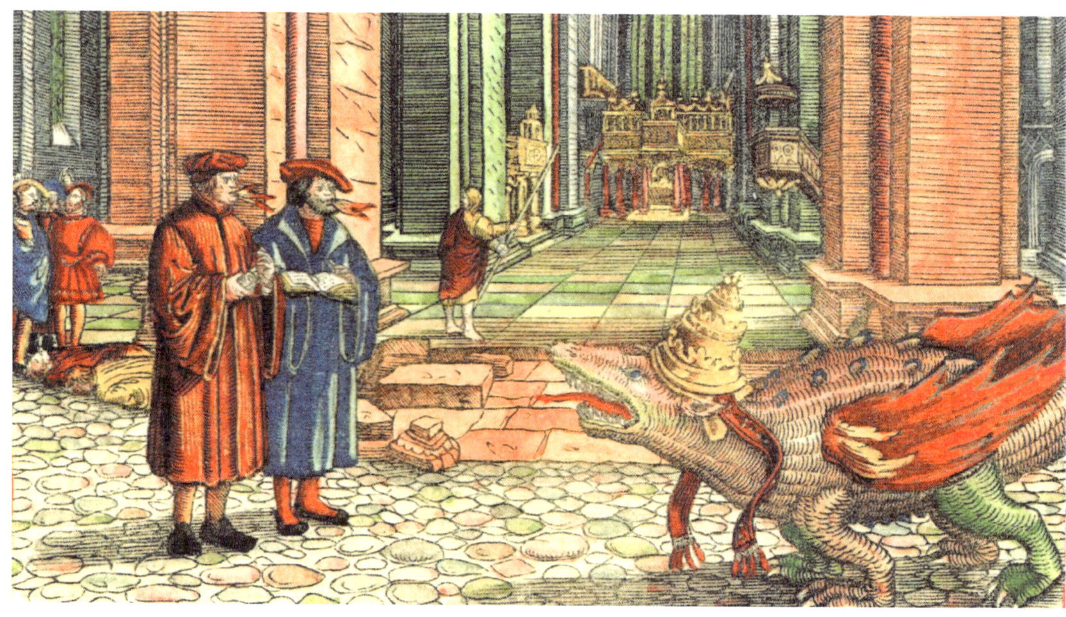

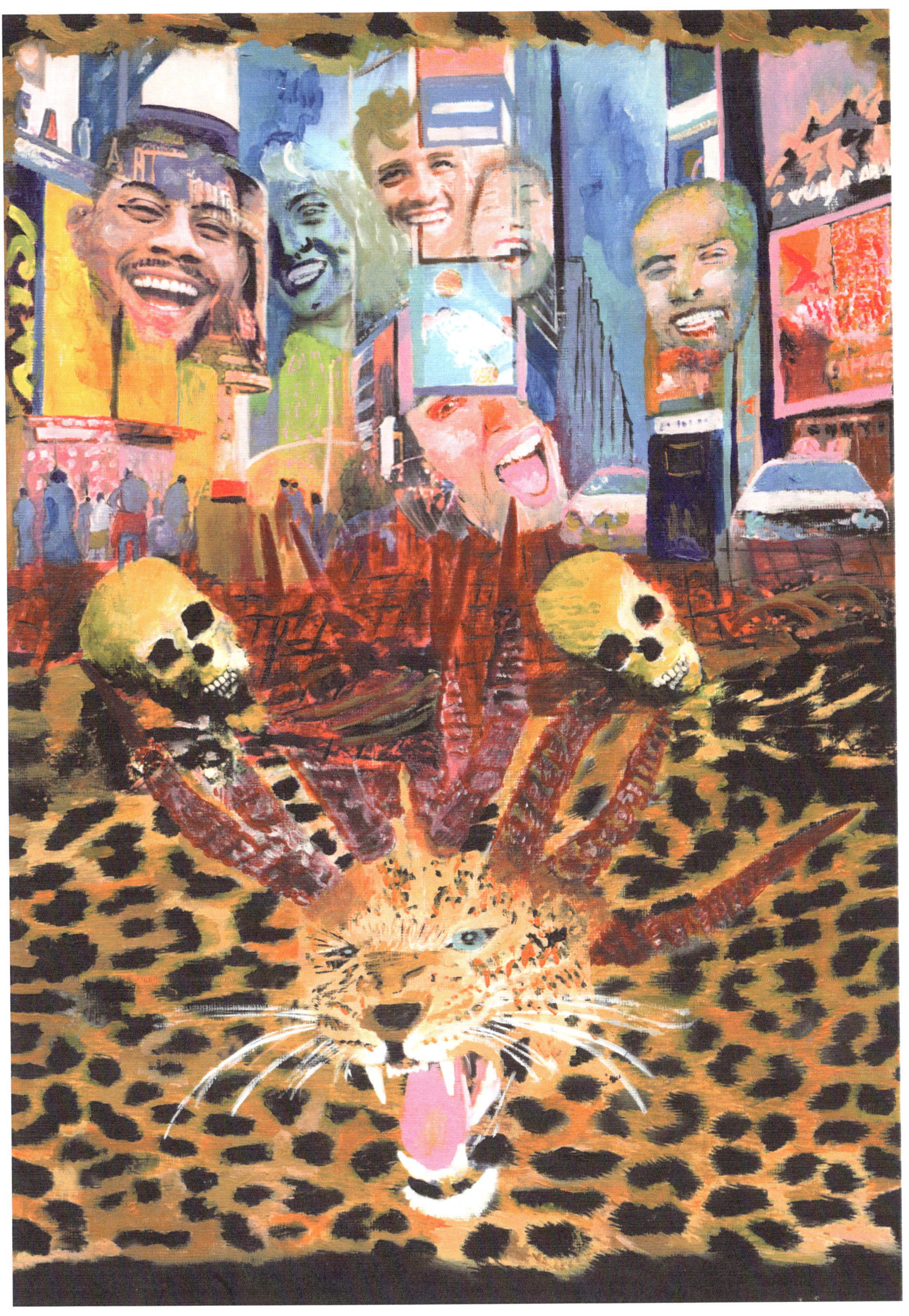

Resurrection and Ascension

Something unexpected happens in the great city, so that the second woe ends on a very triumphant note for the faithful, but a desperate one for the people of the earth. A great public reversal takes place: the witnesses are raised from the dead and ascend to heaven.

> *11: [11]But after the three and a half days, the breath of life from God entered them, and they stood on their feet, and those who saw them were terrified. [12]Then they heard a loud voice from heaven saying to them, "Come up here!" And they went up to heaven in a cloud while their enemies watched them. [13]At that moment there was a great earthquake, and a tenth of the city fell; seven thousand people were killed in the earthquake, and the rest were terrified and gave glory to the God of heaven. [14]The second woe has passed. The third woe is coming very soon.*

The "breath of life" here reminds us of the Genesis account of Adam's creation. By God's intervention, the martyred witnesses stand on their feet and those who see it are terrified. The loud (trumpet?) voice from heaven calls: "Come up!" And they ascend, as Jesus did, but here in full view of their enemies.

As at the death of Jesus, there is an earthquake: "At that moment the curtain of the temple was torn in two, from top to bottom. The earth shook and the rocks were split. The tombs also were opened, and many bodies of the saints who had fallen asleep were raised. After his resurrection they came out of the tombs and entered the holy city and appeared to many. Now when the centurion and those with him who were keeping watch over Jesus, saw the earthquake and what took place, they were terrified and said, 'Truly this man was God's Son!'" (Matt 27:51–54).

The *Getty* has a truly delightful image, with John watching from outside, measuring(?) rod in hand. The breath of God is interpreted as Holy Spirit doves, and we see feet disappearing into the cloud. The angel raises his hand. On the right we see terrified people and a falling city with many dead.

In my painting I quote three drawings by Dunstan Massey, to celebrate and honour his life in this vision of victory.

The second woe is over, but there is one more woe to come as we wait for the seventh, and last, trumpet.

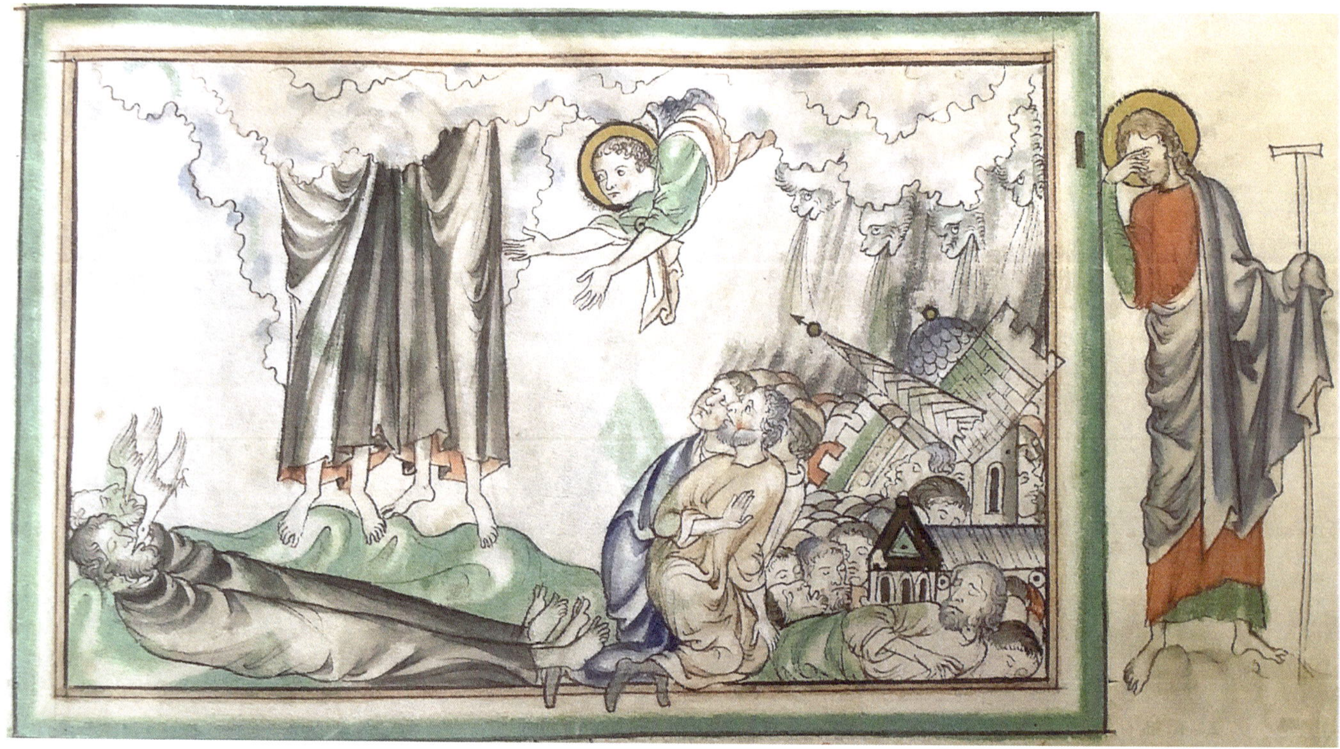

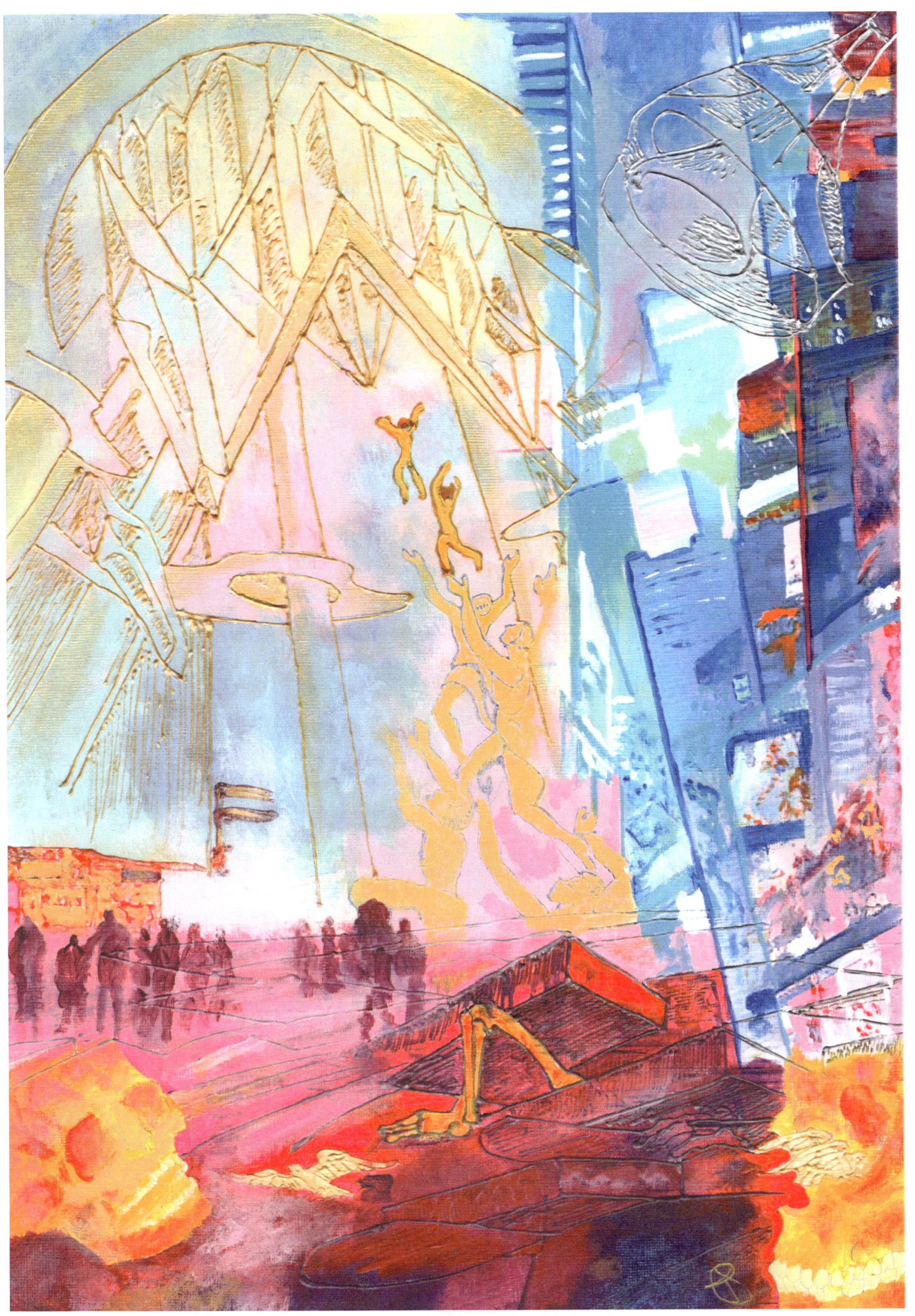

The Seventh Trumpet

The sounding of this last trumpet is not a single vision, but introduces a long series of visions up to and including the end (Beckwith). It starts with a liturgy of praise. This is the "last trumpet" that other NT scriptures mention. The "mystery of God" is about to be revealed (as promised in 10:7).

The third woe will still come "soon", in 12:12!

Where does this worship take place? This takes place in heaven. The *Getty* below places John and the Trumpet angel on a mountain, looking into heaven. There God/Christ, framed in the mandorla that indicates a holy space, holds an open book.

My painting also assumes that this happens in heaven, where (still) very noisy worship continues (as before I use the symbol of four trumpets to indicate the great volume of sound of the voices, and not of trumpets in particular).

The final Trumpet angel now blows his trumpet. I created two colour blocks to symbolise judgement and reward. The elders are crowding around the bejewelled throne. Many commentators mention that this last trumpet initiates a new Yom Kippur, or day of Atonement, a day of forgiveness. Others see this as the start of the final day of the Lord, and I agree with them.

The kingdom of the world has now become the kingdom of our Lord Jesus, for ever. The elders fall down from their thrones onto their faces to worship, and so should we. God is now, "who are and who were" (no longer "to come"). He reigns. The future has come!

11: 15 Then the seventh angel blew his trumpet, and
there were loud voices in heaven, saying,
"The kingdom of the world has become the kingdom
of our Lord
and of his Messiah,
and he will reign forever and ever."
16 Then the twenty-four elders who sit on their thrones
before God fell on their faces and worshiped God,
17 singing,
"We give you thanks, Lord God Almighty,
who are and who were,
for you have taken your great power
and begun to reign.
18 The nations raged,
but your wrath has come,
and the time for judging the dead,
for rewarding your servants, the prophets
and saints and all who fear your name,
both small and great,
and for destroying those who destroy the earth."

His wrath and destruction responded to the rage of the nations (Ps 2).

But His great reward is for the martyrs, the prophets, the saints, for all those who fear him: the small and the great, men, women, girls and boys.

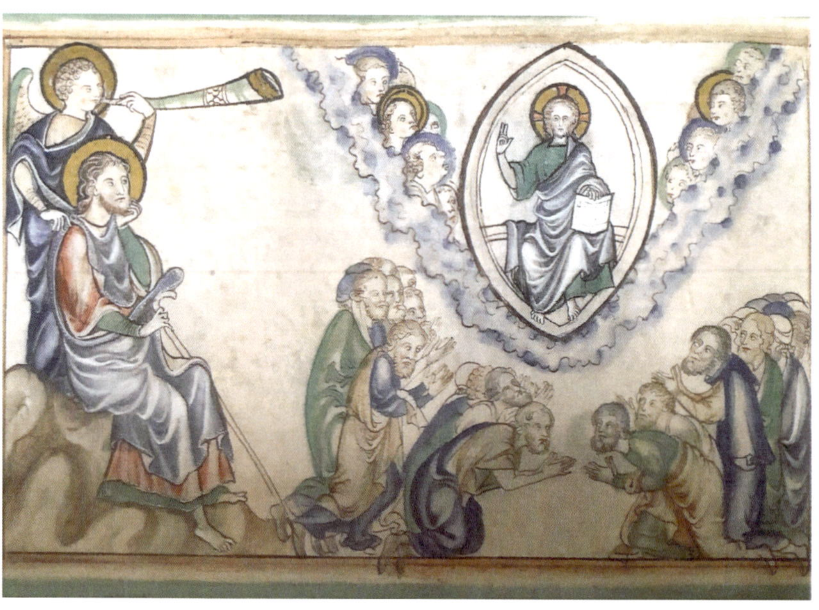

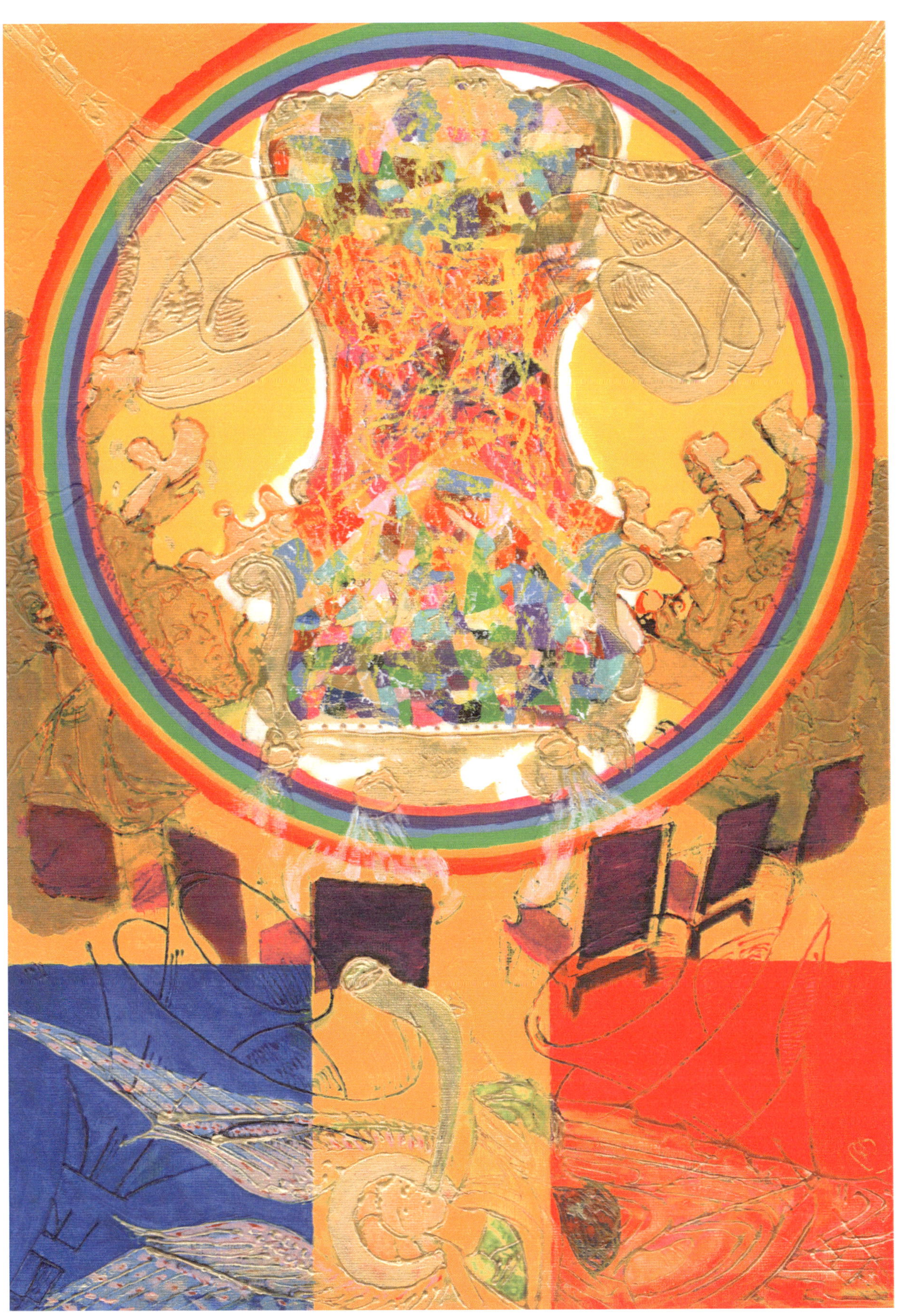

The Ark of His Covenant

> *11: [19]Then God's temple in heaven was opened, and the ark of his covenant was seen within his temple; and there were flashes of lightning, rumblings, peals of thunder, an earthquake, and heavy hail.*

We are looking at God's heavenly temple again (see 11:1). We are reminded of the opening of the door in Revelation 4. And, just as the temple curtain was torn when Jesus died to give access to all into God's holy presence, so God's temple is now opened for the witnesses and all who have come to fear God. That contrasts with access to the holy of holies in the OT, where only the high priest was allowed to enter, once a year, on the day of Atonement after the seventh trumpet blast!

For the only time in Revelation, the ark is seen and mentioned. Its opening is accompanied with flashes of lightning, rumblings, peals of thunder, earthquake and heavy hail. We have come across these signs before: we are on "holy ground". Through John's eyes, we have "seen" the temple, the altars, and now "see" the most holy of all, the ark of the covenant.

There is a difference in opinion whether this appearing of the ark "closes" Revelation 11 or belongs to Revelation 12, or both, as suggested by Smalley.

I like this *Getty* below so much that I quoted it in my own painting! I love its "humanised" winds keeping the ark in the air. The fact that the temple "escapes" from the frame of the illustration is brilliant and delightful!

In my own painting I more clearly distinguish heaven and earth, which shows the effect of the quake. I left the *Getty* illustration intact, but changed its colours. It is more difficult to go "outside the frame" in my book than in the smaller book illustration (I wish I could!). So I concentrated especially on the lightning and hail, with three trumpets indicating a significant level of volume.

To me, this "final" appearance of the ark, symbolises the end of the old covenant and the start of the new.

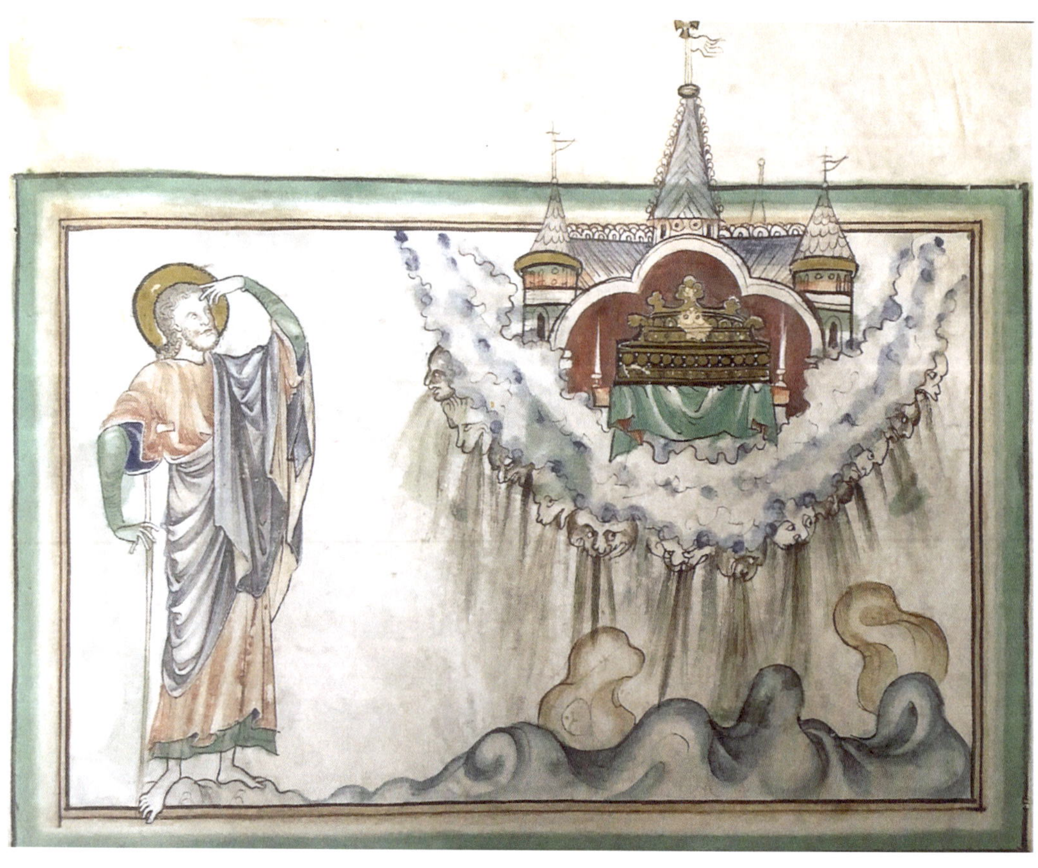

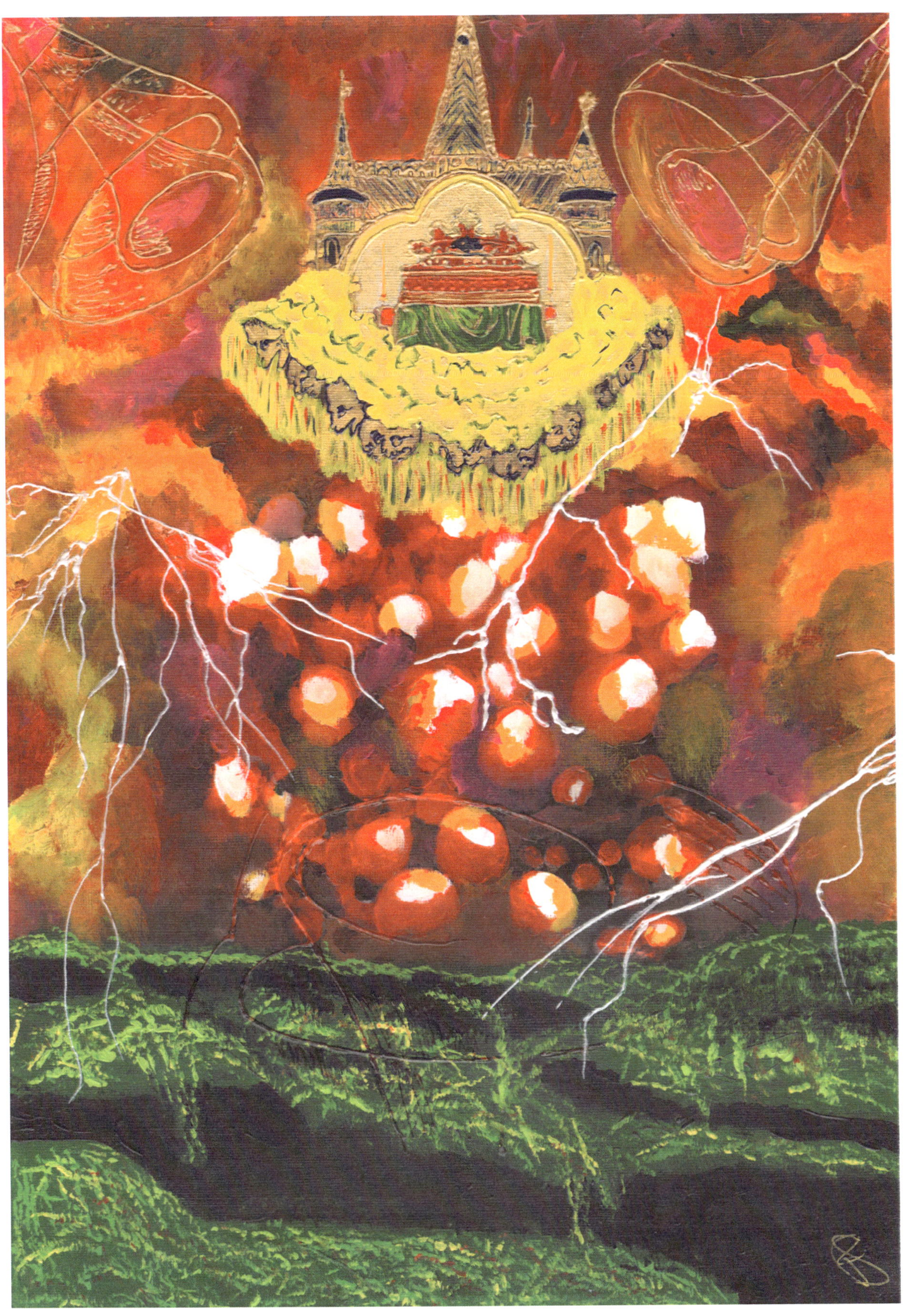

My Understanding of Trumpets, Scroll and Witness

We started with an open heaven, an open scroll and complete silence in heaven, during which John sees an altar appearing in front of the throne. There an angel burns much incense, mixing it with the prayers of all the saints, including the martyrs under the altar (that we read about in Story Twenty-Seven). This prayer-and-incense mixture rises before God and apparently initiates an extraordinary and supernatural sequence of actions and events, from heaven to earth. At the same time, seven angels, having been given a trumpet each, take up position, ready to sound their instruments. Next, burning coals are thrown to the earth by the angel of the Altar as a prophetic action that indicates what we can expect as each trumpet sounds. It seems to be the setting for this whole section of John's vision (with two later mentions of the altar that remind us of this).

The first four trumpets form a clear unit, very similar to the four riders at the opening of the first four seals, but also very different. The horsemen at the seals represented the advance of the gospel and its universal and inevitable effects. The sound of trumpets announces divine action, war, destruction and, ultimately, also calls to worship. Here in response to the trumpets, partial judgement comes, to bring the people of the earth to their senses and to repentance.

The earth, the sea, the rivers, the springs of water, the sun, the moon and the stars are targeted by heaven in an act of partial de-creation. Noah's covenant, the covenant with the whole of creation, is shaken. These are early warnings of what is to come if there is no return to God. They echo the judgements of Exodus, the "plagues" here affecting unbelievers and believers alike (the churches were called to repentance as well). The fact that repentance is still possible may explain the partial destruction (one third).

The three woes introduced by the eagle after the sounding of the fourth trumpet are of a different nature. They are clearly addressed to the people of the earth, the enemies of God.

The fifth trumpet and the first woe open the abyss to release all that is unholy in the spirit world. Demons appear under the leadership of Abaddon. In light of the presence of the altar (8:2) and the fact that Christ holds the key to Hades (1:18), I see this as an angel of God opening the abyss. Everything here happens under God's control. When I read about "composite locusts" let loose to torture but not kill, it reminds me of Job and how God allowed Satan to do his worst, yet safeguarded Job's life. The demons' main tools are lies and deception!

At the sound of the sixth trumpet (Story Forty-Two), the voice from the altar instructs the Trumpet angel to release the four bound angels, who are ordered to kill, apparently in response to the prayers of the martyrs and all God's people. A precise time has been prepared for this judgement on earth, although it is not a time we can calculate. How it comforts us to know God has set an exact time when he will act to set the world to rights!

The second woe is often seen by modern commentators as repeating the first, but I think Leithart is right to see the "hippo-lions" as coming not from the abyss, but from heaven, for only holy things are measured and numbered. The two "myriads" also echo the angelic "myriads" mentioned in 5:11. So, having first opened the abyss, God now opens heaven to release angelic armies, perhaps similar to the angel armies in the visions of Elisha in the OT? This very large heavenly host is commanded to kill a third of the people of the earth, yet those who survive do not repent but cling to their idols of gold, silver, wood and stone.

The second woe continues, in response to these unrepentant people, with another vision. A mighty (huge) angel is seen descending from heaven, with one foot on the earth and the other on the sea, and holding a small, open scroll. The angel appears as a Christ-like figure, possibly the angel of the Lord mentioned in 1:1. He is doing "the revealing" here, and tells John to take and eat. This symbolic language indicates that John is charged to prophesy what is in the scroll, in the spirit of Ezekiel and Jeremiah. Along with Bauckham and many others, I am convinced that this small scroll is identical to the closed scroll mentioned in Story Twenty (Rev 5). It seems natural to expect the contents of the open scroll to be revealed next, and it is, from Revelation 11 onwards.

John also heard what the seven thunders had to say, but it was apparently for him only and not to be recorded. "Is a trumpet blown in a city, and the people are not afraid? Does disaster befall a city, unless the Lord has done it? Surely the Lord God does nothing, without revealing his secret to his servants the prophets" (Amos 3:6); "But in these last days he has spoken to us by a Son, whom he has appointed heir of all things, through whom he also created the worlds" (Heb 1: 2). We do not need to know what the thunders said, and perhaps it is good to be put in our place, to be reminded that this revelation is not recorded to satisy our curiosity!

The angel then swears an oath that when the seventh trumpet sounds, time will be no more! I am not convinced this means "no delay" as some interpret it, but rather that time will be no more. God's mystery will be fulfilled. This mystery is much discussed and certainly includes Gentiles becoming heirs with Israel and sharers in the promise in Christ through the gospel (Eph 3:3–6). But it could also, and more likely, refer to the mystery mentioned by Paul concerning the marriage between Jesus and His church (Eph 5:32).

By eating the scroll, John is commissioned as prophet. He has to internalise the message so that it becomes literally part of him. It tastes sweet and bitter, sweet in experiencing the presence of God but bitter in some of the effects of preaching the gospel (persecution, judgement on the world...).

The second woe continues. John sets to work as prophet by measuring the temple of God, the altar and those who worship there, but not the outer courts, given to the Gentiles, who will trample them for 42 months. This period is the same as the period in which the two witnesses do their work.

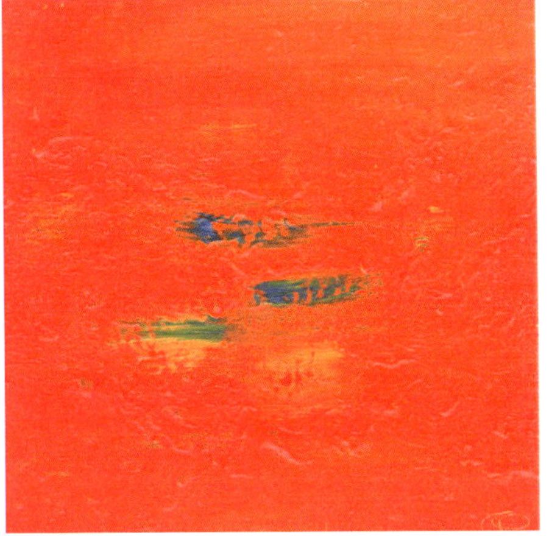

The two witnesses remind us of Jesus, Moses and Elijah, Jeremiah and the prophets, Peter and Paul, and the living church. They witness until their work is done. Then, like Jesus, they are killed, by the beast.

But death cannot hold them, just as it could not hold Jesus, and they are resurrected after three and a half days to ascend to heaven. Their persecutors and killers repent, apparently with remorse, but many commentators have rightly questioned this repentance. This also happened at Jesus' crucifixion, after which the centurion repented (Matt 27:54) and others also were struck with a deep sense of sorrow about what they had been part of (Luke 23:48). The second woe is over now.

Commentators are right to recognise that the literary structure of Revelation 11 around the 42 months, 1260 days and 3.5 days links this chapter to Revelation 12–14, as a kind of introduction, as Boxall suggests.

Finally, the seventh and last trumpet is sounded, and this time to our surprise, it is a call to worship! The "last" day of human history begins with a worship liturgy. The third woe is imminent but does not officially begin with the sound of the seventh trumpet; instead, we have to wait until 12:12. The trumpet does begin the day of the Lord, as I consider it to be, and all that follows reveals the contents of the scroll, the mystery of God, the judgements that result from the third woe and the rewards for those who persevered. The kingdom has come on earth as it is in heaven; God's will is done on earth as in heaven; the Lord's Prayer is fulfilled. This indeed is the meaning of the last trumpet (1 Cor 15:52).

As the veil of the temple was torn from top to bottom when Jesus died (Mark 15:38), so here the temple in heaven is opened and the ark of the covenant is seen, with lightning, rumblings, thunder, earthquakes and hail (signs that accompanied God's appearance at Sinai in the OT). The meaning of this is discussed by the writer to the Hebrews (12:18-25): the end of the old covenant. John now has direct access to God. And, as we shall see, so do we!

What do we make of this narrative of the trumpets? It seems to me there are several levels of understanding it: the heavenly, the cosmic, the earthly, but also the spiritual.

Heaven and earth are shown to be closely related in Revelation. The trumpets sound in heaven, and the actions initiated in heaven have consequences on earth (and in heaven). The witnesses work on earth, where they are killed, but then ascend to heaven. Believers will recognise what is happening here, for it has happened before, to Jesus, and is happening to his people now, and will continue to happen...

The battles are spiritual battles, "not against flesh and blood but against the powers" (Eph 6), against spiritual rulers fuelling worldly ideology, politics and idolatry. In this context, we are shown that His people are sealed at all times, as witnesses to the living God.

There is also a great cosmic element here, especially shown in the first four trumpets, for God is capable of shaking the earth, sea and luminaries in partial dissolution of His covenant with Noah.

How should we respond to all this? Pray! And pray! And love God, His earth and its people, while there is time. God is moved by prayer of all His people and of the martyrs, sweetened by the incense of the intercessions of Jesus. So there is much we can be busy with, at all times and everywhere, as prayer has hands and feet too!

The day of the Lord has been announced. But it is not yet the end of what John will be shown. We are only halfway through the Book of Revelation! Without a break, John's vision runs on into much more, and surprising, details.

Visual Meditation 3: Light in Colour

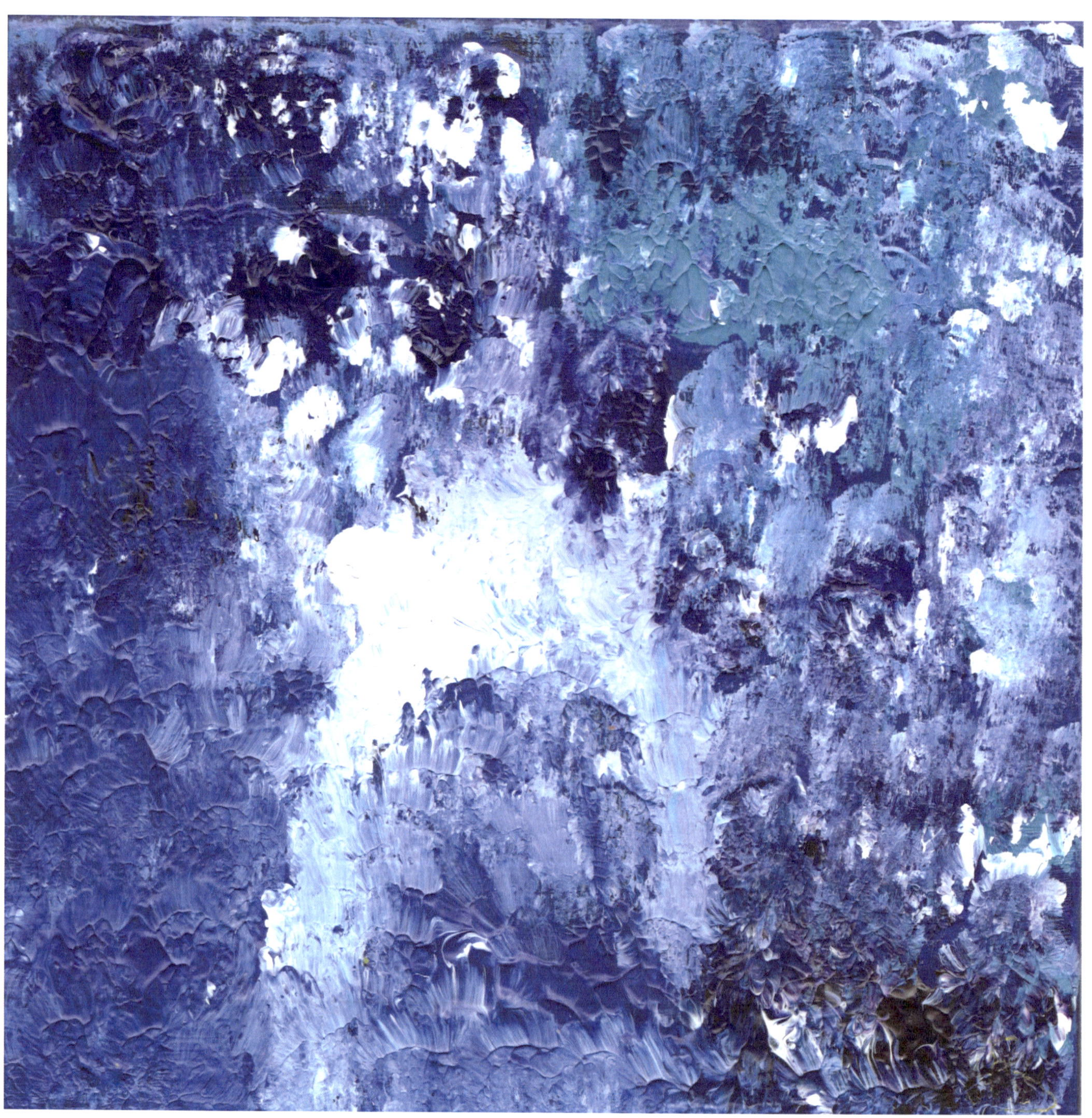

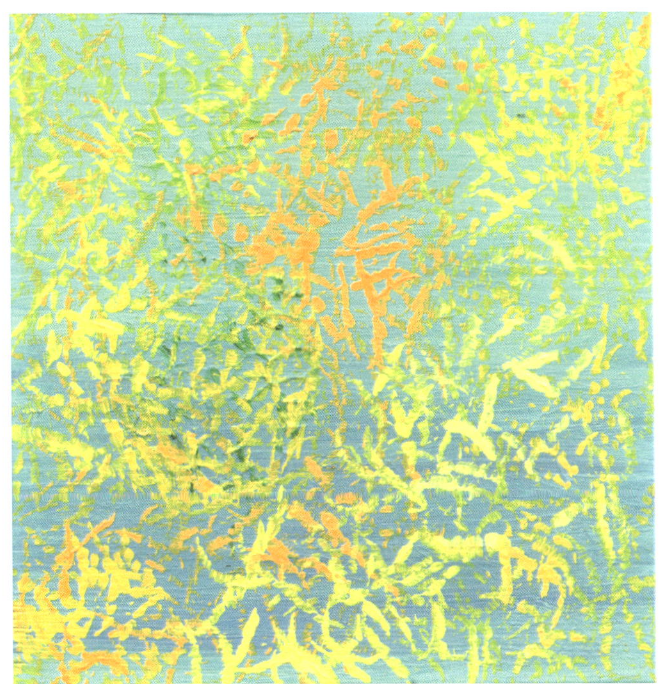

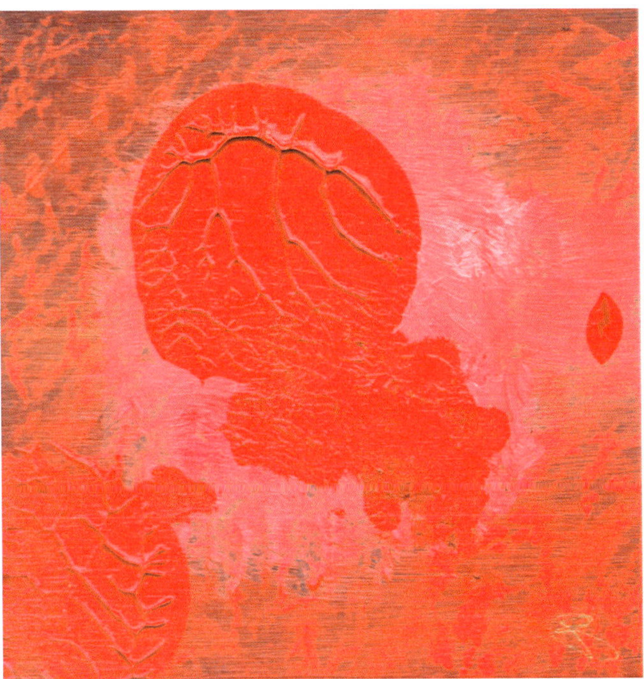

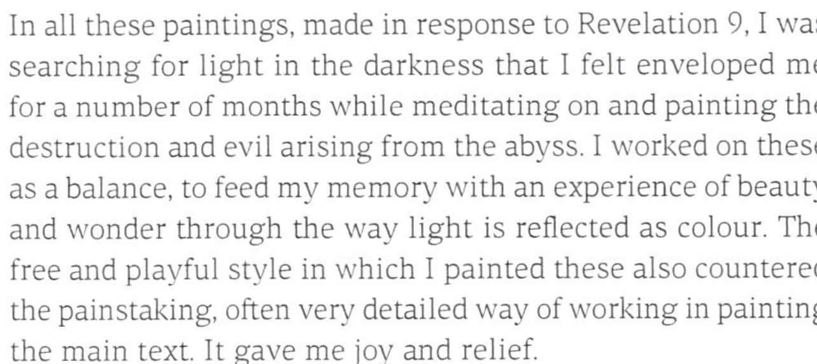

In all these paintings, made in response to Revelation 9, I was searching for light in the darkness that I felt enveloped me for a number of months while meditating on and painting the destruction and evil arising from the abyss. I worked on these as a balance, to feed my memory with an experience of beauty and wonder through the way light is reflected as colour. The free and playful style in which I painted these also countered the painstaking, often very detailed way of working in painting the main text. It gave me joy and relief.

During this time, my work was happily disturbed by a visit from my grandchildren Saoirse and Jonah who were keen to "do some painting with Opa". Watching them make their colourful creations inspired my two small paintings below, from using the leftover paint on their palettes, Saoirse left and Jonah right. These are my prayer for the preservation and guidance of God for all the very young growing up today. I was struck by how much Revelation 9 is also about light, about God's committed love and implemented plan for keeping His children safe through onslaughts!

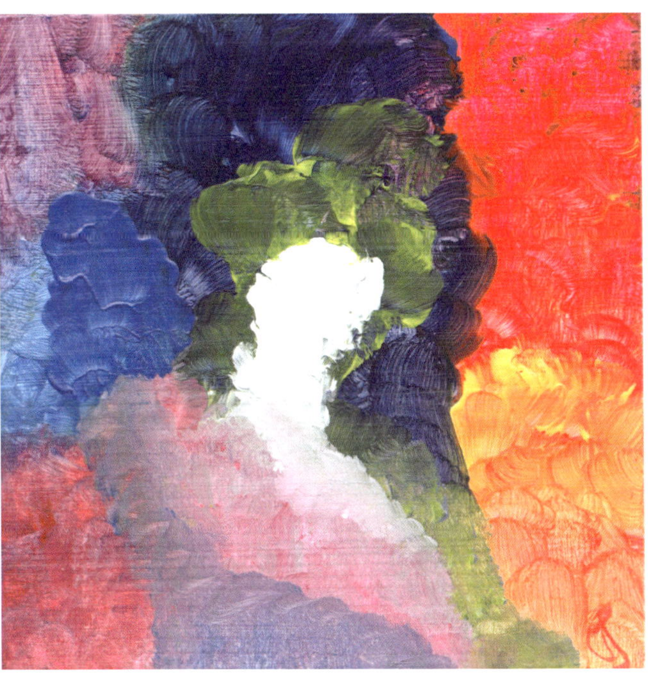

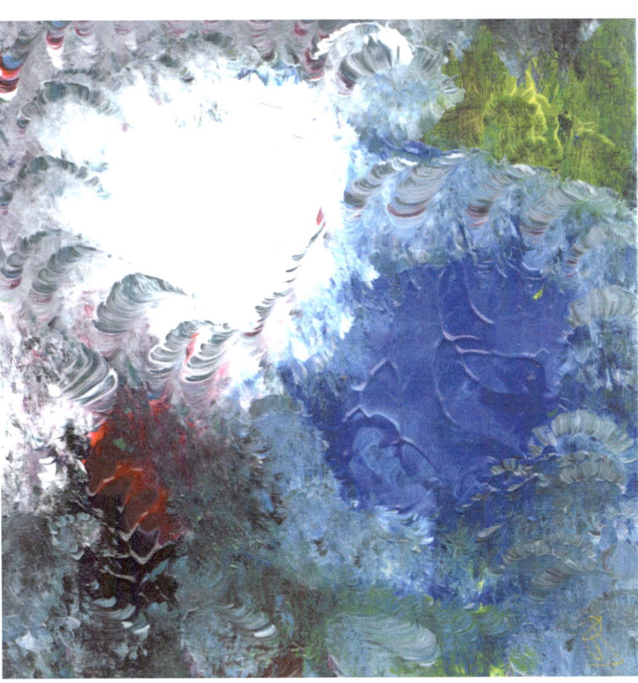

Additional Select Further Reading

For preachers and church leaders

Grabiner, Steven Charles. 2015. *Revelation's Hymns: Commentary on the Cosmic Conflict*. London: Bloomsbury T&T Clark.

Osborne, Grant R. 2016. *Revelation Verse by Verse*. Bellingham, WA: Lexham Press.

Poythress, Vern S. 2000. *The Returning King: A Guide to the Book of Revelation*. Phillipsburg, NJ: P&R.

Rossetti, Christina Georgina. 1893. *The Face of the Deep: A Devotional Commentary on the Apocalypse*. 2nd ed. London: SPCK.

Sweet, J. P. M. 1979. *Revelation*. London: SCM Press.

Wainwright, Arthur William. 1993. *Mysterious Apocalypse : Interpreting the Book of Revelation*. Nashville: Abingdon Press.

For serious students and theologians

Abir, Peter Antonysamy. 1995. *The Cosmic Conflict of the Church: An Exegetico-Theological Study of Revelation 12:7-12*. Frankfurt am Main: Peter Lang.

Beckwith, Isbon Thaddeus. 2001. *The Apocalypse of John: studies in introduction, with a critical and exegetical commentary*. Eugene, OR: Wipf & Stock.

Bernier, Jonathan. 2022. *Rethinking the Dates of the New Testament: The Evidence for Early Composition*. Grand Rapids, MI: Baker Academic a division of Baker Publishing Group.

Court, John M. 1979. *Myth and History in the Book of Revelation*. London: SPCK.

Fekkes, Jan. 1988. *Isaiah and Prophetic Traditions in the Book of Revelation: Visionary Antecedents and Their Development*. University of Manchester.

Gay, Meg. "Monumental Apocalypse Cycles of the 14th century"; A dissertation submitted for the degree of Doctor of Philosophy, University of York Centre for Medieval Studies, Sept 1999.

Jauhiainen, Marko. *'apokaluyis ihsou cristou' (rev. 1:1): The climax of John's prophecy?* Academia.

Jauhiainen, Marko. *The measuring of the sanctuary reconsidered (rev 11,1-2)*, cat.inist.fr, Biblica, 2002, Academia.

Jauhiainen, Marko. *Recapitulation and Chronological Progression in John's Apocalypse: Towards a New Perspective*, New Test. Stud. 49, pp. 543–559. Cambridge University Press.

Jauhiainen, Marko. *The Use of Zechariah in Revelation*. Mohr Siebeck, 2019.

Lee, Chee-Chiew. "Fire from their mouths" Academia

McNicol, Allan J. 2012. *The Conversion of the Nations in Revelation*. Paperback ed. 1st published ed. London: Bloomsbury.

Peels, H.G.L . 2023. *Storm Over De Wereld; De Volkenprofetieën Van Het Boek Jeremia*. Utrecht: KokBoekencentrum Uitgevers.

Petersen, Rodney Lawrence. 1993. *Preaching in the Last Days: The Theme of "Two Witnesses" in the Sixteenth and Seventeenth Centuries*. New York: OUP.

Rissi, Mathias. 1972. *The Future of the World: an Exegetical Study of Revelation 19.11-22.15*. Expanded and rev. version of the orig. German ed. London: SCM Press.

Siew, Antoninus King Wai. 2005. *The War between the Two Beasts and the Two Witnesses: A Chiastic Reading of Revelation 11:1-14:5*. London: T&T Clark.

Smith, Robert. "Songs of the Seer." *Themelios* 43.2 (2018:193-194).

Turner, Seth. "Revelation 11:1-13 History of Interpretation". DPhil in Theology, St John's College.

For art lovers

Emmerson, Richard Kenneth. 1981. *Antichrist in the Middle Ages: A Study of Medieval Apocalypticism Art and Literature*. Print ed. Manchester Univ. Press.

Hommel-Steenbakkers, Nelly de, A. M. Koldeweij, Miró Mónica and Ruth Koenig. 2005. *Flemish Apocalypse*. Barcelona: Moleiro.

Liśkiewicz, Izabela, Richard Kenneth Emmerson, Peter Kidd, Britt Boler Hunter and M. Moleiro, Editor S.A. 2020. *Picture Book of the Life of St John and the Apocalypse*.

Kort, Kees de. 1989. *Amos, een profeet uit Juda*. Haarlem: Nederlands Bijbelgenootschap.

Massey, Dunstan. 2017. *The Mystic Mountain: a poetic scenario for the Resurrection with other poems*. Piquant Edition.

Miró Vinaixa, Mònica. 2020. *The Val-Dieu Apocalypse*. Barcelona: M. Moleiro.

Moleiro, Manuel, Anne Barton de Mayor, Nigel Morgan, Suzanne Lewis, Aires Nascimento, Michelle P. Brown and Raquel Somoano. 2019. *Gulbenkian Apocalypse* = Apocalipsis Gulbenkian.

Praet, Danny and Maximiliaan P. J. Martens. 2019. *The Ghent Altarpiece*: van Eyck. Art History Science and Religion. Veurne Belgium: Hannibal Publishing.

Sleigh, Daphne, and Melva McLean. 2013. *The Artist in the Cloister: the life and works of Father Dunstan Massey*.

Strine, C. A., Mark McInroy, Alexis Torrance, J. M. F. Heath, Robin Margaret Jensen and Vittorio Montemaggi. 2021. *Image As Theology: The Power of Art in Shaping Christian Thought Devotion and Imagination*. Turnhout Belgium: Brepols.

Van Gogh, Vincent, and Nicholas Wadley. 1969. *The Drawings of Van Gogh*. London: Hamlyn.

List of Illustrations

By Pieter Kwant

By Other Artists

10, 16, 18, 20, 32, 40, 42, 44, 46, 48 From the *Dyson Perrins Apocalypse. MS Ludwig III 1* (Getty Museum). Creative Commons Licence CC01.0

12 From the *Silos Beatus*. MS 11695 (The British Library, London). Copyright © M. Moleiro, S.A., 2019.

14, 24, 26, 28 From the *Rylands Beatus*. Copyright © The University of Manchester, 2021. Used with permission.

Table of Contents

www.ingramcontent.com/pod-product-compliance
Lightning Source LLC
LaVergne TN
LVRC090924100826
845154LV00013B/159

* 9 7 8 1 8 0 3 2 9 0 1 1 9 *